Journaling for Spirit, Soul & Body

Scriptural Writing Prompts for Women

By Dawnis Edge

This written record of thoughts, dreams, ideas, goals, objectives, tangents, disappointments, hurts, triumphs, tragedies, celebrations, challenges, and discoveries belongs to:

. . . . ● ● ● ● ● ● ● ● . . . . .

This journal belongs to you. It is a catalog of your day, week, month or year. It can be written in everyday...or not. It can be started in January...or not. It's yours. Make it work for you. It is not how often you write, but that you write. It's a record of a time in space of the mundane things in life, the exciting things, the hurtful things, the things you overcame, the things you want to remember.

Your journey in your journal. You may find it helpful to review every year. You may find a healing in just telling your story, writing it down and never revisiting it.

Use it in a way that works for you. It's designed to give guidance, make you think and ponder, but ultimately, if you don't use it in a way that works for you, you won't use it.

"Write the vision, make it plain so that he who reads it may run with it." Habakkuk 2:2

You are made of spirit, soul and body.

Your spirit is the part of you which has always been and will always be.

Your soul is your mind, your will and your emotions.

Your body is what your soul and spirit are housed in.

You are a spirit, you possess your soul and live in a body.

Each of these needs to be taken care of.

On the first page of each day is a space for each of these categories. Write your plan to feed these parts of yourself.

For your body it may be drink more water, exercise or simply rest.

Your soul needs feeding in a different way. It can be fed by reading a book, taking a walk, solving a problem, making personal connections, increasing knowledge base or getting to the root of a problem.

Your spirit gets feed by reading and meditating on the Word of God, praise, and worshiping Him. Each day has a scripture and an opportunity to write what it is saying to you in that moment. Personal scripture application may change depending on the current circumstances in your life.

The facing page is lined. They are for you to pour out of your spirit, mind, will and emotions, thoughts, ideas, dreams and goals. What do you hear in your spirit? What do you feel? What do you see? What's life like in this moment?

Write a lot. Write a little. Write often. Write less frequently. But do write.

Date: _____

Spirit:

Trust in the Lord with all your heart, do not depend on your own understanding; in all your ways submit to him and he will make your paths straight. Proverbs 3:5-6 NLT

Today, for me, this means:

_____

_____

_____

_____

Soul: Today I will feed my soul by:

_____

_____

_____

_____

Body: Today I will feed by body by:

_____

_____

_____

_____

_____

Date: _____

Spirit: _____

For the kingdom of God is not a matter of eating or drinking, but of righteousness, peace and joy in the Holy Spirit. Romans 14:17 NIV

Today, for me, this means:

_____

_____

_____

_____

_____

Soul: Today I will feed my soul by:

_____

_____

_____

Body: Today I will feed by body by:

_____

_____

_____

_____

_____

Date: _____

Spirit: _____

Dear friends, let us love one another, for love comes from God. Everyone who loves has been born of God and knows God. 1 John 4:7 NIV

Today, for me, this means:

_____

_____

_____

_____

_____

Soul: Today I will feed my soul by:

_____

_____

_____

_____

Body: Today I will feed by body by:

_____

_____

_____

_____

Date: _____

Spirit:

Don't you realize that all of you together are the temple of God and that the Spirit of God lives in you? 1 Corinthians 3:16 NLT

Today, for me, this means:

_____
_____
_____
_____
_____
_____

Soul: Today I will feed my soul by:

_____
_____
_____

Body: Today I will feed by body by:

_____
_____
_____
_____

Date: _____

Spirit:

Do not conform to the pattern of this world, but be transformed by the renewing of your mind. then you will be able to test and approve what God's will is~his good, pleasing and perfect will. Romans 12:2 NIV

Today, for me, this means:

_____
_____
_____
_____

Soul: Today I will feed my soul by:

_____
_____
_____

Body: Today I will feed by body by:

_____
_____
_____
_____
_____

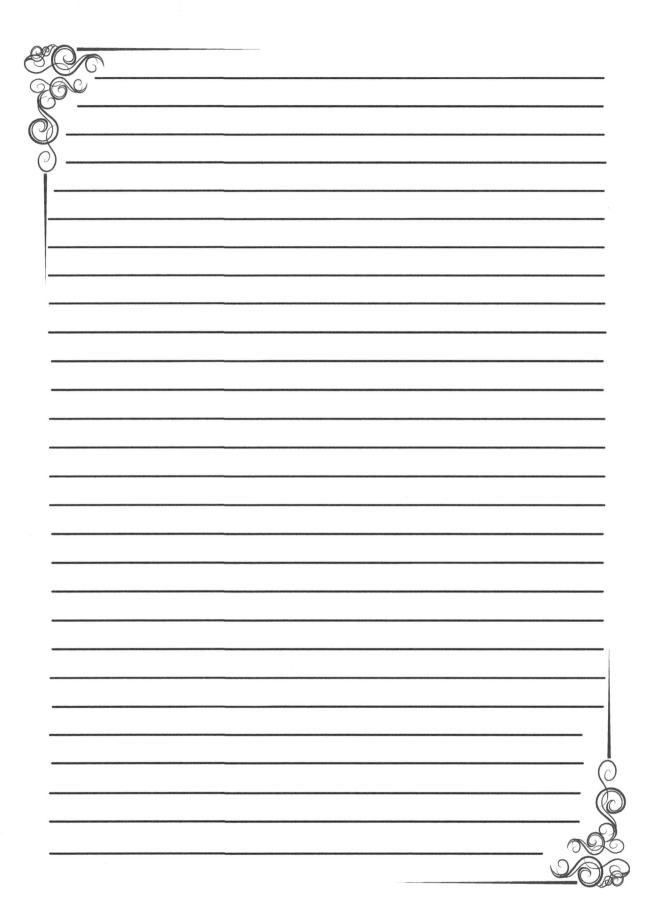

Date: _____

Spirit:

My heart has heard you say, "Come and talk with me." and
my heart responds, "Lord, I am coming." Psalm 27:8 NLT

Today, for me, this means:

_____
_____
_____
_____
_____
_____

Soul: Today I will feed my soul by:

_____
_____
_____

Body: Today I will feed by body by:

_____
_____
_____
_____

Date: _____

Spirit:

And it is impossible to please God without faith. Anyone who wants to come to him must believe that God exists and that he rewards those who sincerely seek him. Hebrews 11:6 NLT

Today, for me, this means:

_____

_____

_____

_____

_____

Soul: Today I will feed my soul by:

_____

_____

_____

Body: Today I will feed by body by:

_____

_____

_____

_____

_____

Date: _____

Let all that I am praise the Lord; with my whole heart, I
will praise his holy name. Psalm 103:1 NLT

Today, for me, this means:

_____

_____

_____

_____

_____

_____

Soul: Today I will feed my soul by:

_____

_____

_____

_____

Body: Today I will feed by body by:

_____

_____

_____

_____

_____

Date: _____

A peaceful heart leads to a healthy body; jealousy is like cancer in the bones. Proverbs 14:30 NLT

Today, for me, this means:

_____
_____
_____
_____
_____

Soul: Today I will feed my soul by:

_____
_____
_____
_____

Body: Today I will feed by body by:

_____
_____
_____
_____

Date: _____

Spirit: _____

—— • ——

Jesus replied, "You must love the Lord your God with all your heart, all your soul, and all your mind." Matthew 22:37 NLT

—— • ——

Today, for me, this means:

_____
_____
_____
_____
_____

Soul: Today I will feed my soul by:

_____
_____
_____
_____

Body: Today I will feed by body by:

_____
_____
_____
_____
_____

Date: _____

Spirit:

So letting your sinful nature control your mind leads to death. But letting the Spirit control your minds leads to life and peace. Romans 8:6 NLT

Today, for me, this means:

_____

_____

_____

_____

_____

Soul: Today I will feed my soul by:

_____

_____

_____

_____

Body: Today I will feed by body by:

_____

_____

_____

_____

Date: _____

For I have given rest to the weary and joy to the sorrowing.

Jeremiah 31:25 NLT

Today, for me, this means:

_____
_____
_____
_____
_____

Soul: Today I will feed my soul by:

_____
_____
_____
_____

Body: Today I will feed by body by:

_____
_____
_____
_____
_____

Date: _____

He fills my life with good things. My youth is renewed like
the eagle's. Psalm 103:5 NLT

Today, for me, this means:

_____

_____

_____

_____

_____

Soul: Today I will feed my soul by:

_____

_____

_____

Body: Today I will feed by body by:

_____

_____

_____

_____

_____

Date: _____

Spirit:

◆ •◆ •◆

Dear friend, I pray that you may enjoy health and that all may go well with you, even as your soul is getting along well. 3 John 1:2 NIV

◆ •◆ •◆

Today, for me, this means:

_____
_____
_____

_____

_____

Soul: Today I will feed my soul by:

_____
_____
_____
_____

Body: Today I will feed by body by:

_____
_____
_____
_____
_____

Date: _____

But you desire honesty from the womb, teaching me wisdom even there. Psalm 51:6 NLT

Today, for me, this means:

_____

_____

_____

_____

_____

Soul: Today I will feed my soul by:

_____

_____

_____

Body: Today I will feed by body by:

_____

_____

_____

_____

Date: _____

Spirit:

But you, O Lord, are a shield around me; you are my glory,
the one who holds my head high. Psalm 3:3 NLT

Today, for me, this means:

_____

_____

_____

_____

_____

Soul: Today I will feed my soul by:

_____

_____

_____

_____

Body: Today I will feed by body by:

_____

_____

_____

_____

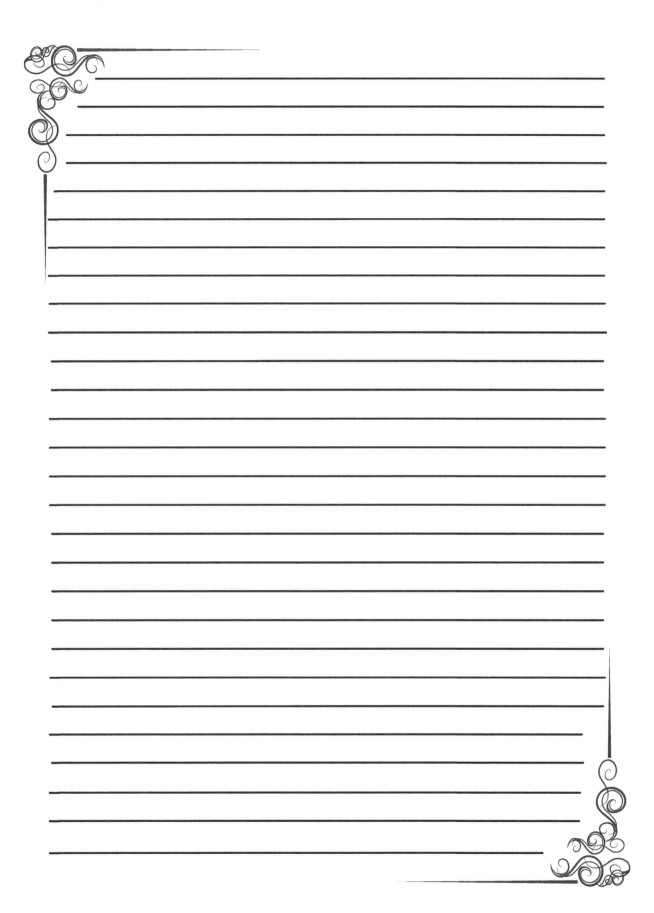

Date: _____

So whether you eat or drink or whatever you do, do it all for the glory of God. 1 Corinthians 10:31 NIV

Today, for me, this means:

_____

_____

_____

_____

_____

_____

Soul: Today I will feed my soul by:

_____

_____

_____

_____

Body: Today I will feed by body by:

_____

_____

_____

_____

Date: _____

But those who hope in the Lord will renew their strength. They will soar on wings like eagles; they will run and not grow weary, they will walk and not be faint. Isaiah 40:31 NIV

Today, for me, this means:

_____

_____

_____

_____

Soul: Today I will feed my soul by:

_____

_____

_____

Body: Today I will feed by body by:

_____

_____

_____

_____

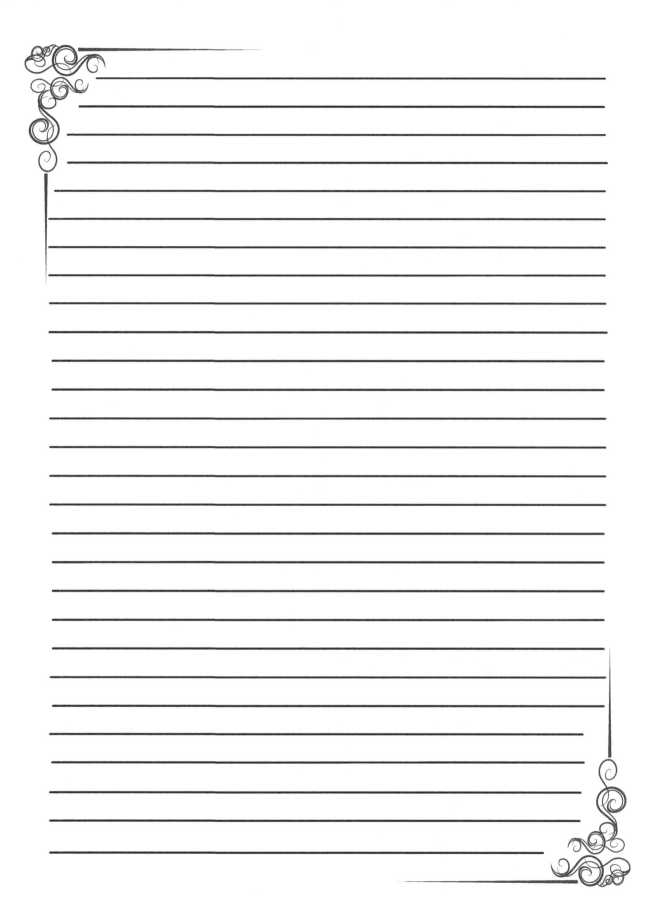

Date: _____

Spirit:

God is spirit, and his worshippers must worship in the Spirit
and in truth. John 4:24 NIV

Today, for me, this means:

_____
_____
_____
_____
_____

Soul: Today I will feed my soul by:

_____
_____
_____
_____

Body: Today I will feed by body by:

_____
_____
_____
_____
_____

Date: _____

Spirit:

For physical training is of some value, but godliness has value for all things, holding promise for both present life and the life to come.

1 Timothy 4:8 NIV

Today, for me, this means:

_____

_____

_____

_____

_____

Soul: Today I will feed my soul by:

_____

_____

_____

_____

Body: Today I will feed by body by:

_____

_____

_____

_____

Date: _____

Spirit:

———◆●◆———

You were bought at a price. Therefore honor God with your
bodies. 1 Corinthians 6:20 NIV

———◆●◆———

Today, for me, this means:

_____

_____

_____

_____

_____

Soul: Today I will feed my soul by:

_____

_____

_____

Body: Today I will feed by body by:

_____

_____

_____

_____

_____

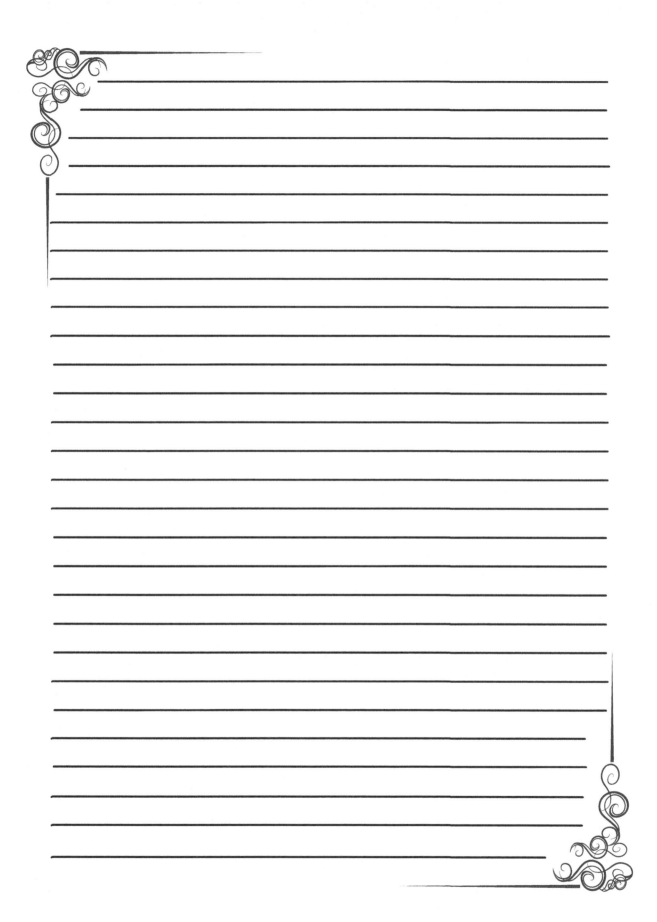

Date: _____

Therefore we do not lose heart. Though outwardly we are
wasting away, yet inwardly we are being renewed day by day.

2 Corinthians 4:16 NIV

Today, for me, this means:

_____

_____

_____

_____

Soul: Today I will feed my soul by:

_____

_____

_____

_____

Body: Today I will feed by body by:

_____

_____

_____

_____

_____

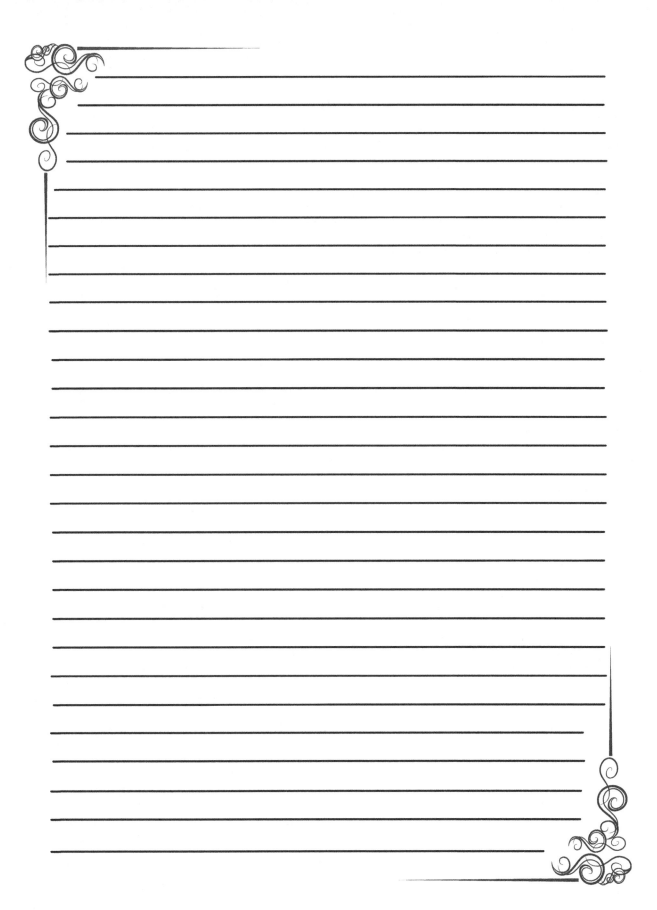

Date: _____

Spirit:

For he satisfies the thirsty and fills the hungry with good things.
Psalms 107:9 NLT

Today, for me, this means:

_____
_____
_____
_____
_____
_____

Soul: Today I will feed my soul by:

_____
_____
_____
_____

Body: Today I will feed by body by:

_____
_____
_____
_____

Date: _____

Since God chose you to be the holy people he loves, you must clothe yourselves with tenderhearted mercy, kindness, humility, gentleness, and patience.   Colossians 3:12 NLT

Today, for me, this means:

_____

_____

_____

_____

Soul: Today I will feed my soul by:

_____

_____

_____

Body: Today I will feed by body by:

_____

_____

_____

_____

Date: _____

You will keep in perfect peace all who trust in you, all whose thoughts are fixed on you! Isaiah 26:3 NLT

Today, for me, this means:

_____

_____

_____

_____

_____

Soul: Today I will feed my soul by:

_____

_____

_____

Body: Today I will feed by body by:

_____

_____

_____

_____

Date: _____

Spirit:

_____◆_____

Since we are living by the Spirit, let us follow the Spirit's leading in every part of our lives. Galatians 5:25 NLT

_____◆_____

Today, for me, this means:

_____

_____

_____

_____

_____

Soul: Today I will feed my soul by:

_____

_____

_____

_____

Body: Today I will feed by body by:

_____

_____

_____

_____

_____

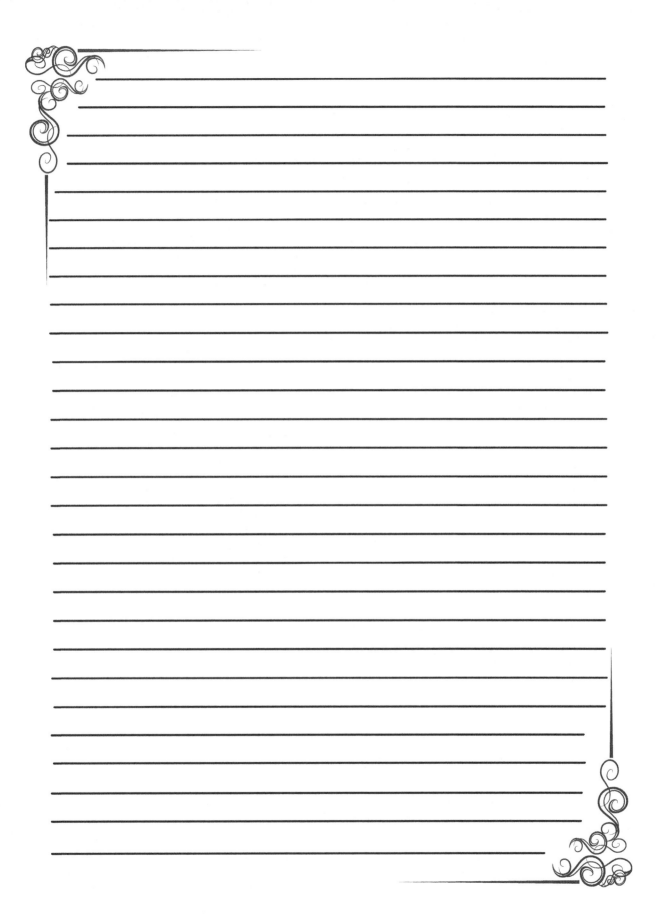

Date: _____

By his divine power, God has given us everything we need for living a godly life. We have received all this by coming to know him, the one who called us to himself by means of his marvelous glory and excellence.

2 Peter 1:3 NLT

Today, for me, this means:

_____

_____

_____

_____

Soul: Today I will feed my soul by:

_____

_____

_____

_____

Body: Today I will feed by body by:

_____

_____

_____

_____

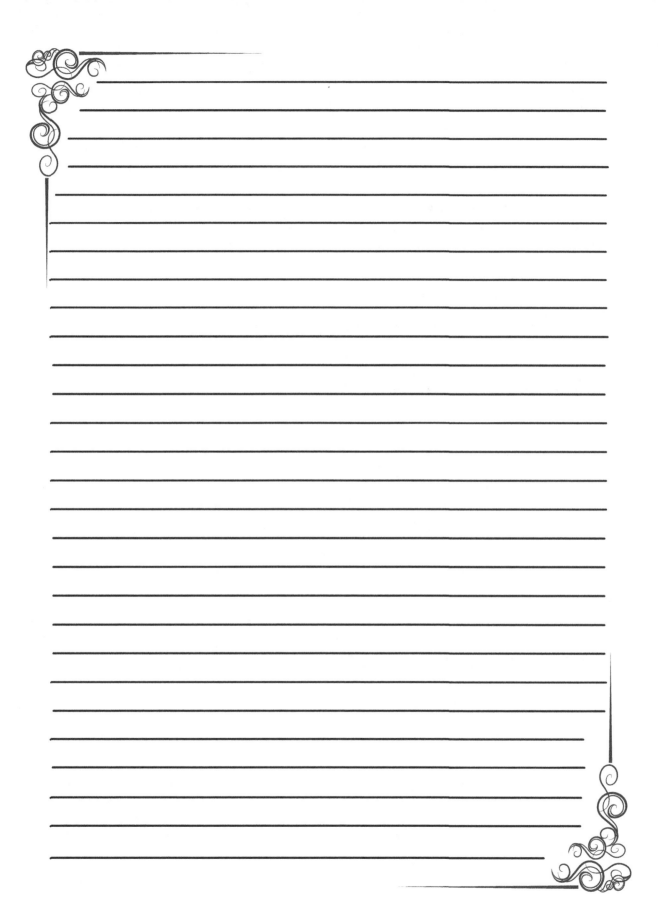

Date: _____

Spirit:

And we are instructed to turn from godless living and sinful pleasures. We should live in this evil world with wisdom, righteousness and devotion to God, Titus 2:12 NLT

Today, for me, this means:

_____
_____
_____
_____

Soul: Today I will feed my soul by:

_____
_____
_____
_____

Body: Today I will feed by body by:

_____
_____
_____
_____
_____

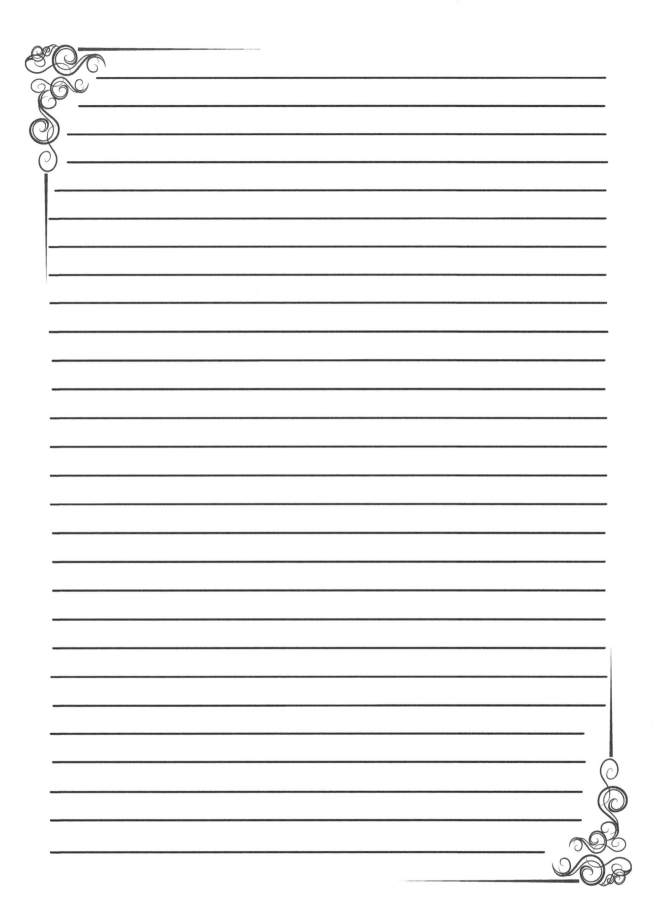

Date: _____

Let us think of ways to motivate one another to acts of love and good works. Hebrews 10:24 NLT

Today, for me, this means:

_____

_____

_____

_____

_____

_____

Soul: Today I will feed my soul by:

_____

_____

_____

Body: Today I will feed by body by:

_____

_____

_____

_____

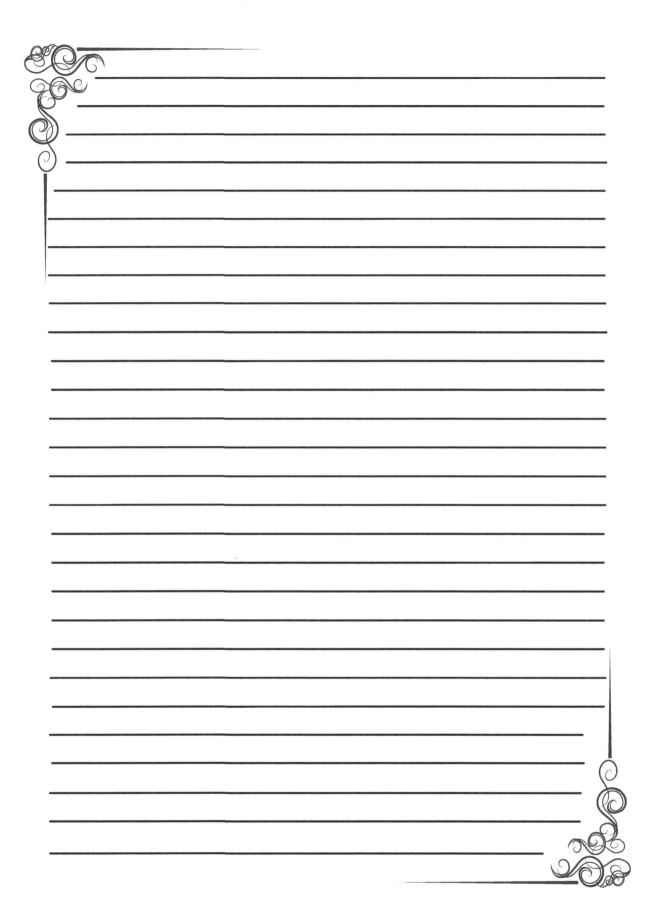

Date: _____

❖ ❖ ❖

God blesses those who hunger and thirst for justice, for they
will be satisfied. Matthew 5:6 NLT

❖ ❖ ❖

Today, for me, this means:

_____

_____

_____

_____

_____

_____

Soul: Today I will feed my soul by:

_____

_____

_____

_____

Body: Today I will feed by body by:

_____

_____

_____

_____

_____

Date: _____

Guard your heart above all else, for it determines the course of your life. Proverbs 4:23 NLT

Today, for me, this means:

_____

_____

_____

_____

_____

Soul: Today I will feed my soul by:

_____

_____

_____

_____

Body: Today I will feed by body by:

_____

_____

_____

_____

_____

Date: _____

Spirit:

---•◆•---

Now may the God of peace make you holy in every way, and may
your whole spirit and soul and body be kept blameless until our
Lord Jesus Christ comes again. 1 Thessalonians 5:23 NLT

---•◆•---

Today, for me, this means:

_____

_____

_____

_____

_____

Soul: Today I will feed my soul by:

_____

_____

_____

_____

Body: Today I will feed by body by:

_____

_____

_____

_____

_____

Date: _____

And what do you benefit if you gain the whole world but lose your own soul? Is anything worth more than your soul? Matthew 16:26 NLT

Today, for me, this means:

_____
_____
_____
_____
_____
_____

Soul: Today I will feed my soul by:

_____
_____
_____
_____

Body: Today I will feed by body by:

_____
_____
_____
_____
_____

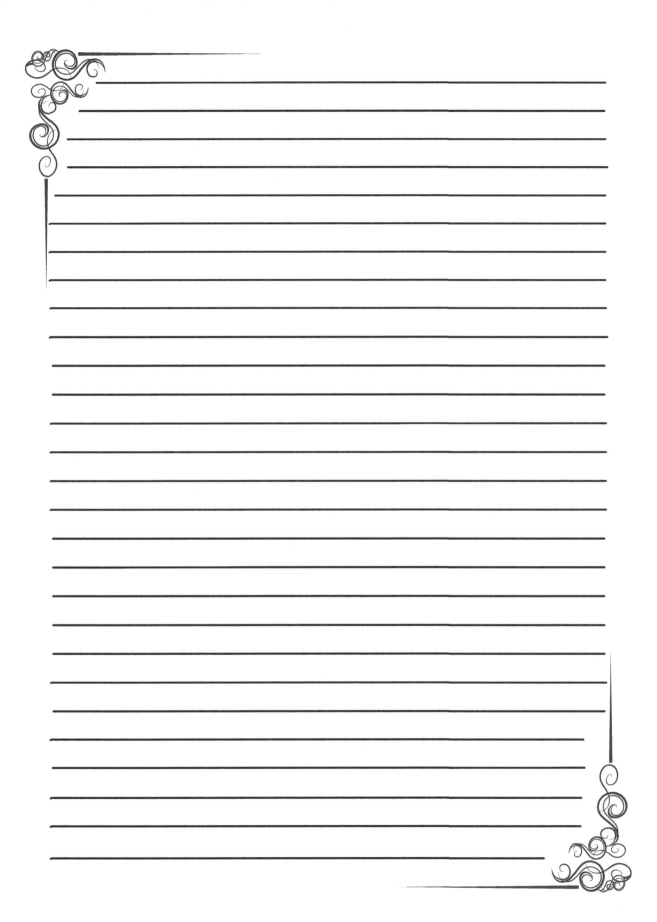

Date: _____

———◆———

They replied, "Believe in the Lord Jesus and you will be saved, along with everyone in your household." Acts 16:31 NLT

———◆———

Today, for me, this means:

_____
_____
_____
_____
_____

Soul: Today I will feed my soul by:

_____
_____
_____
_____

Body: Today I will feed by body by:

_____
_____
_____
_____
_____

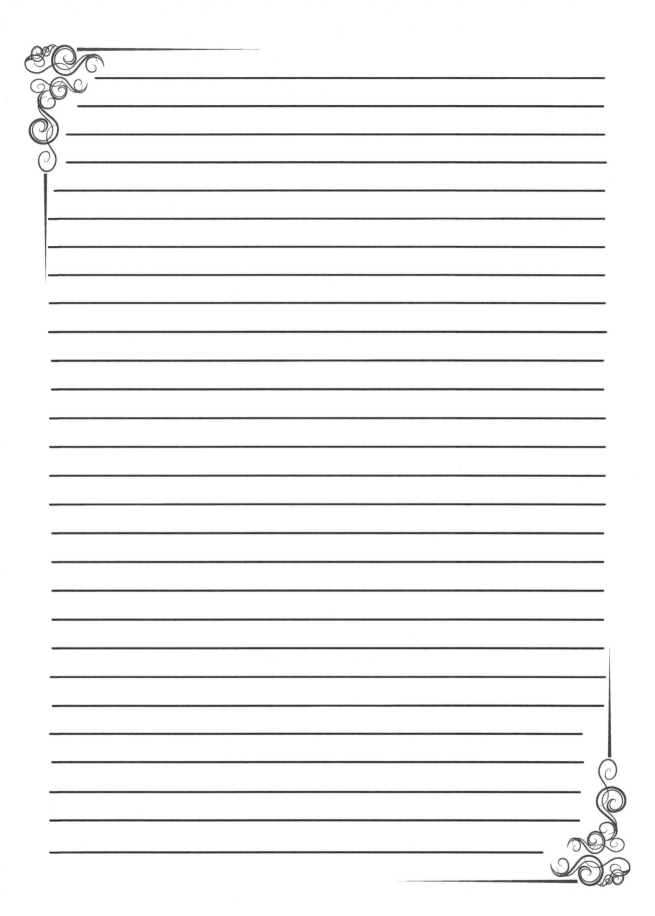

Date: _____

Spirit:

For God has not given us the spirit of fear and timidity, but of power, love, and self-discipline. 2 Timothy 1:7 NLT

Today, for me, this means:

_____

_____

_____

_____

_____

Soul: Today I will feed my soul by:

_____

_____

_____

Body: Today I will feed by body by:

_____

_____

_____

_____

Date: _____

Spirit:

...he saved us, not because of the righteous things we had done, but because of his mercy. He washed away our sins, giving us a new birth and new life through the Holy Spirit. Titus 3:5 NLT

Today, for me, this means:

_____
_____
_____
_____
_____

Soul: Today I will feed my soul by:

_____
_____
_____
_____

Body: Today I will feed by body by:

_____
_____
_____
_____
_____

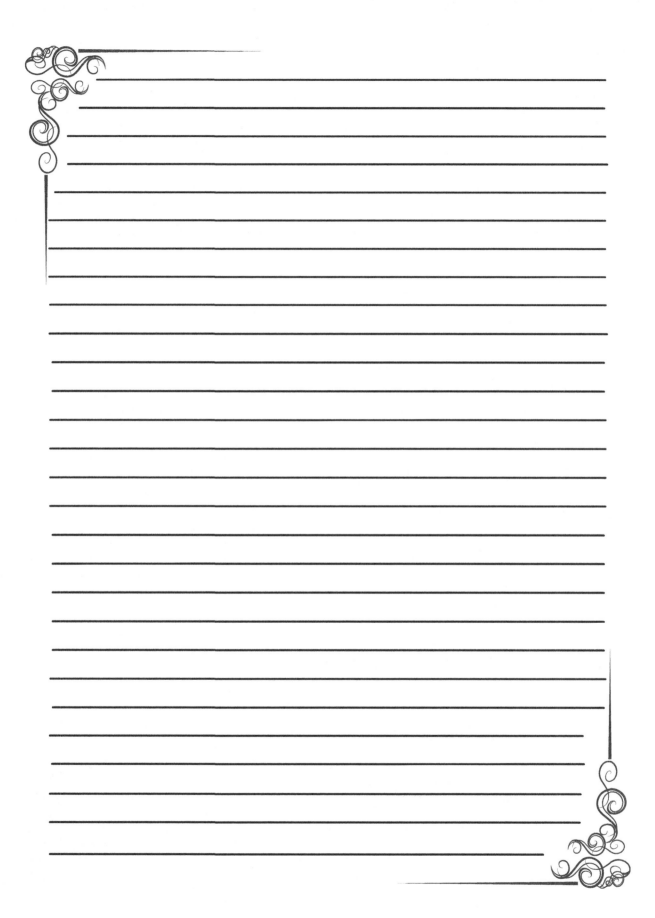

Date: _____

Spirit:

Then the way you live will always honor and please the Lord, and your lives will produce every kind of good fruit. All the while, you will grow as you learn to know God better and better. Colossians 1:10 NLT

Today, for me, this means:

_____
_____
_____
_____
_____

Soul: Today I will feed my soul by:

_____
_____
_____

Body: Today I will feed by body by:

_____
_____
_____
_____
_____

Date: _____

Spirit:

———◆●◆———

Therefore, I urge you, brothers and sisters, in view of God's mercy, to offer your bodies as a living sacrifice, holy and pleasing to God—this is your true and proper worship. Romans 12:1 NIV

———◆●◆———

Today, for me, this means:

_____

_____

_____

_____

Soul: Today I will feed my soul by:

_____

_____

_____

Body: Today I will feed by body by:

_____

_____

_____

_____

_____

Date: _____

<u>Spirit:</u>

—————— • • ——————

For God is the one who provides seed for the farmer and then bread to eat. In the same way, he will provide and increase your resources and then produce a great harvest of generosity in you. 2 Corinthians 9:10 NLT

—————— • • ——————

Today, for me, this means:

_____
_____
_____
_____

<u>Soul:</u> Today I will feed my soul by:

_____
_____
_____
_____

<u>Body:</u> Today I will feed by body by:

_____
_____
_____
_____
_____

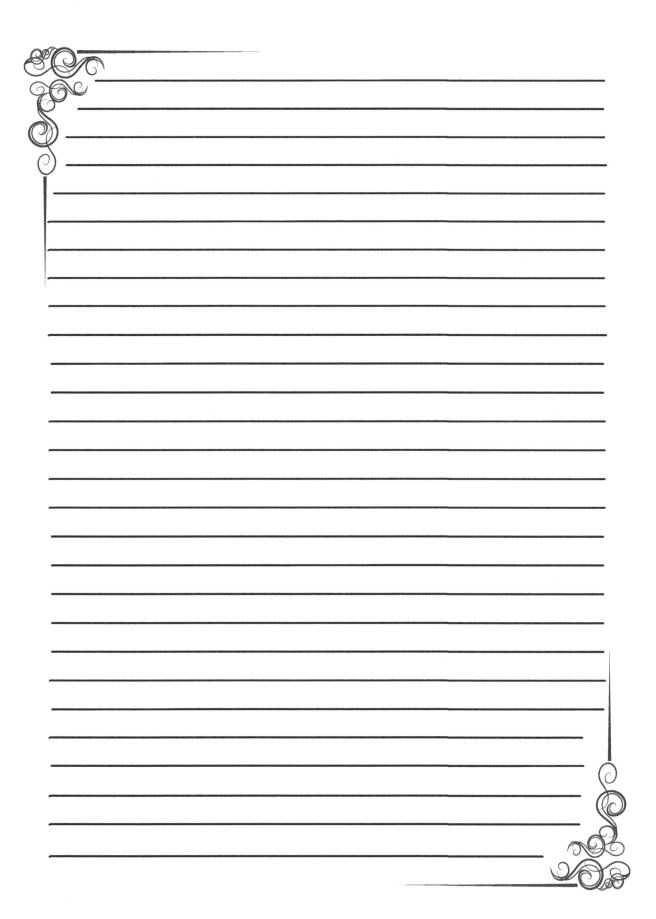

Date: _____

Spirit:

And you must love the Lord your God with all your heart, all your soul, and all your strength. Deuteronomy 6:5 NLT

Today, for me, this means:

_____
_____
_____

_____
_____
_____

Soul: Today I will feed my soul by:

_____
_____
_____
_____

Body: Today I will feed by body by:

_____
_____
_____
_____
_____

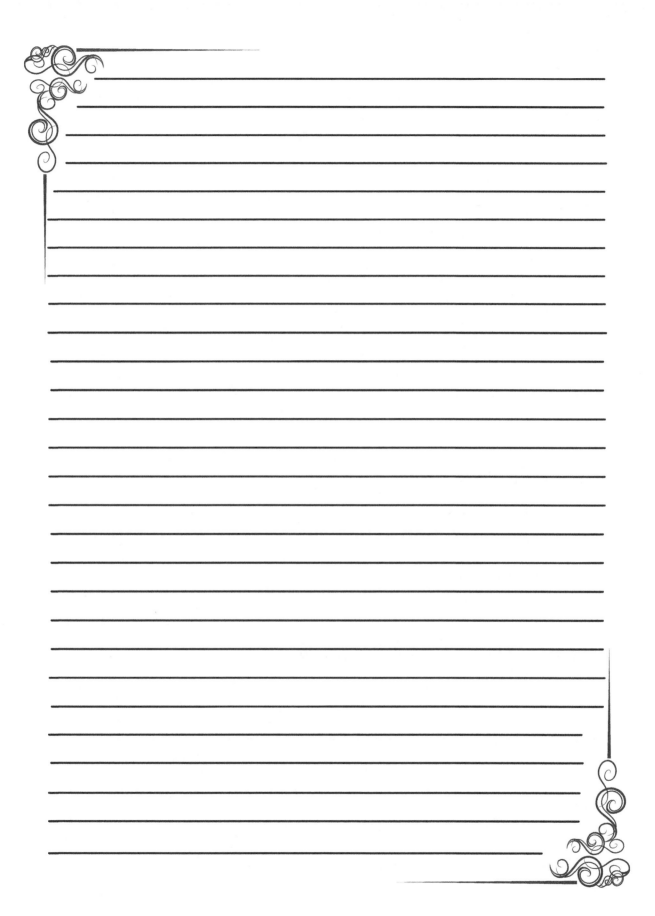

Date: _____

Spirit:

And I am certain that God, who began the good work within you, will continue his work until it is finally finished on the day when Christ returns. Philippians 1:6 NLT

Today, for me, this means:

_____
_____
_____
_____

Soul: Today I will feed my soul by:

_____
_____
_____
_____

Body: Today I will feed by body by:

_____
_____
_____
_____

Date: _____

Spirit:

Ask me and I will tell you remarkable secrets you do not know about things to come. Jeremiah 33:3 NLT

Today, for me, this means:

_____

_____

_____

_____

_____

Soul: Today I will feed my soul by:

_____

_____

_____

Body: Today I will feed by body by:

_____

_____

_____

_____

Date: _____

But they delight in the law of the Lord, meditating on it day and night. Psalm 1:2 NLT

Today, for me, this means:

_____

_____

_____

_____

_____

_____

Soul: Today I will feed my soul by:

_____

_____

_____

_____

Body: Today I will feed by body by:

_____

_____

_____

_____

_____

Date: _____

Let the wise listen to these proverbs and become even wiser. Let those with understanding receive guidance. Proverbs 1:5 NLT

Today, for me, this means:

_____
_____
_____
_____
_____
_____

Soul: Today I will feed my soul by:

_____
_____
_____
_____

Body: Today I will feed by body by:

_____
_____
_____
_____
_____

Date: _____

Spirit:

The Lord is my shepherd; I have all that I need.
Psalm 23:1 NLT

Today, for me, this means:

_____
_____
_____

_____
_____
_____

Soul: Today I will feed my soul by:

_____
_____
_____
_____

Body: Today I will feed by body by:

_____
_____
_____
_____
_____

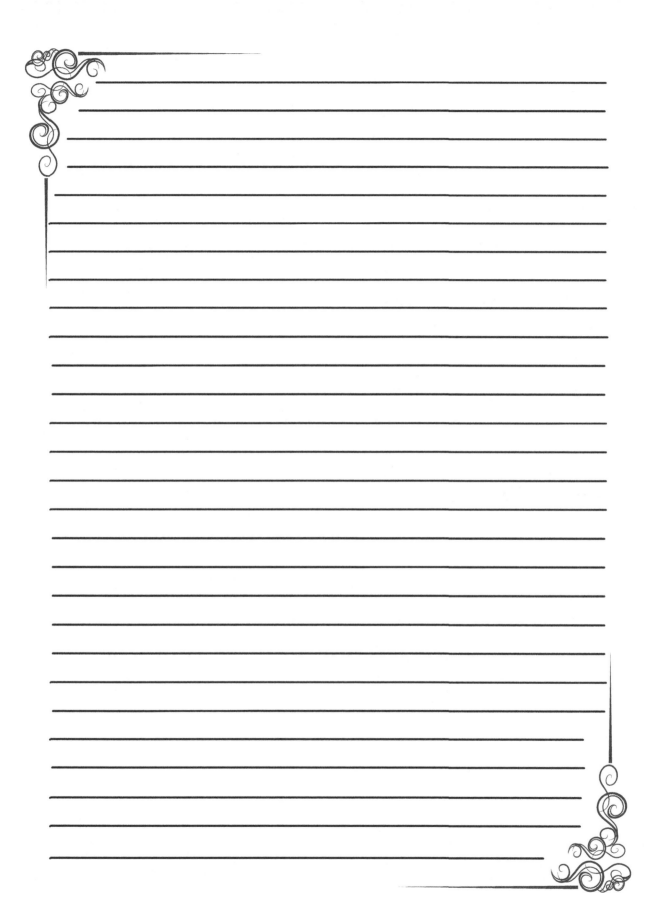

Date: _____

Spirit:

So all of us who have had that veil removed can see and reflect the glory of the Lord. And the Lord—who is the Spirit—makes us more and more like him as we are changed into his glorious image. 2 Corinthians 3:18 NLT

Today, for me, this means:

_____
_____
_____
_____
_____

Soul: Today I will feed my soul by:

_____
_____
_____
_____

Body: Today I will feed by body by:

_____
_____
_____
_____
_____

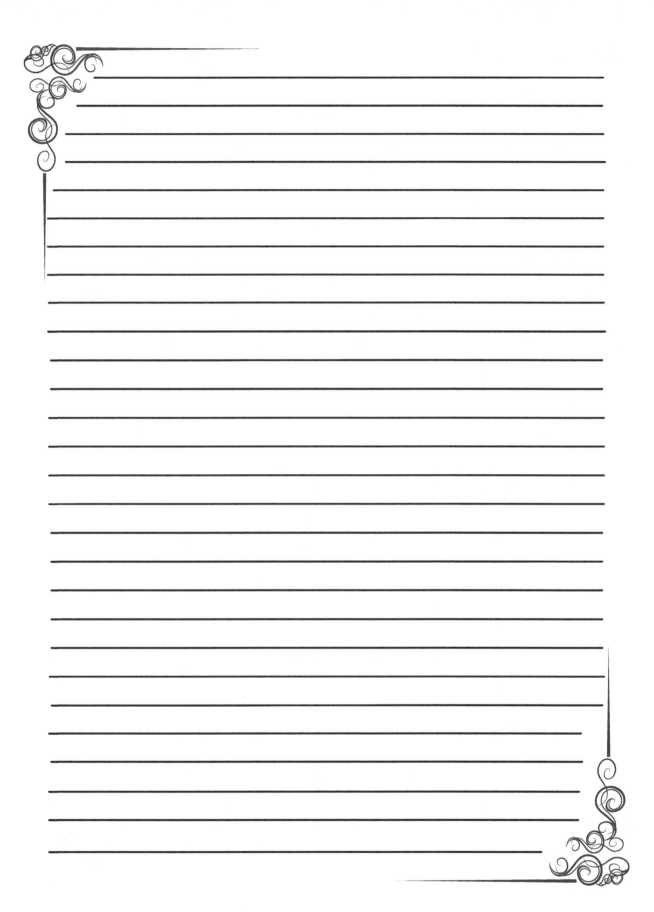

Date: _____

Spirit:

So let it grow, for when your endurance is fully developed, you
will be perfect and complete, needing nothing. James 1:4 NLT

Today, for me, this means:

_____
_____
_____

_____

_____

_____

Soul: Today I will feed my soul by:

_____

_____

_____

Body: Today I will feed by body by:

_____

_____

_____

_____

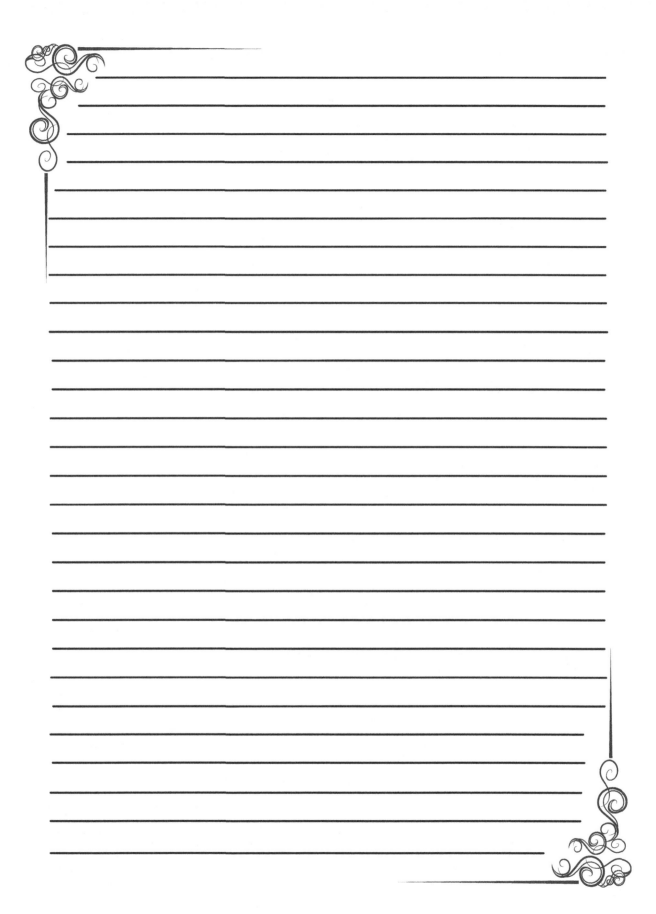

Date: _____

——— ◆ • ◄ ———

The Lord himself will fight for you. Just stay calm.

Exodus 14:14 NLT

——— ◆ • ◄ ———

Today, for me, this means:

_____

_____

_____

_____

_____

_____

Soul: Today I will feed my soul by:

_____

_____

_____

_____

Body: Today I will feed by body by:

_____

_____

_____

_____

_____

Date: _____

> This is my command—be strong and courageous. Do not be afraid or discouraged. For the Lord your God is with you wherever you go.
> Joshua 1:9 NLT

Today, for me, this means:

_____
_____
_____
_____

Soul: Today I will feed my soul by:

_____
_____
_____

Body: Today I will feed by body by:

_____
_____
_____
_____
_____

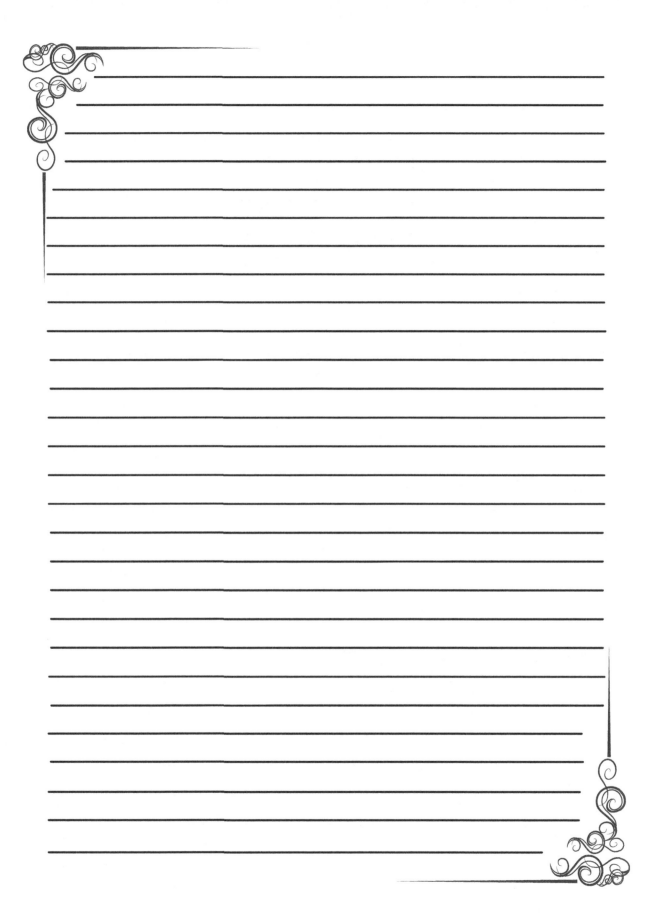

Date: _____

Spirit:

The faithful love of the Lord never ends. His mercies never cease.

Great is his faithfulness; his mercies begin afresh each morning.

Lamentations 3:22-23 NLT

Today, for me, this means:

_____

_____

_____

_____

Soul: Today I will feed my soul by:

_____

_____

_____

Body: Today I will feed by body by:

_____

_____

_____

_____

_____

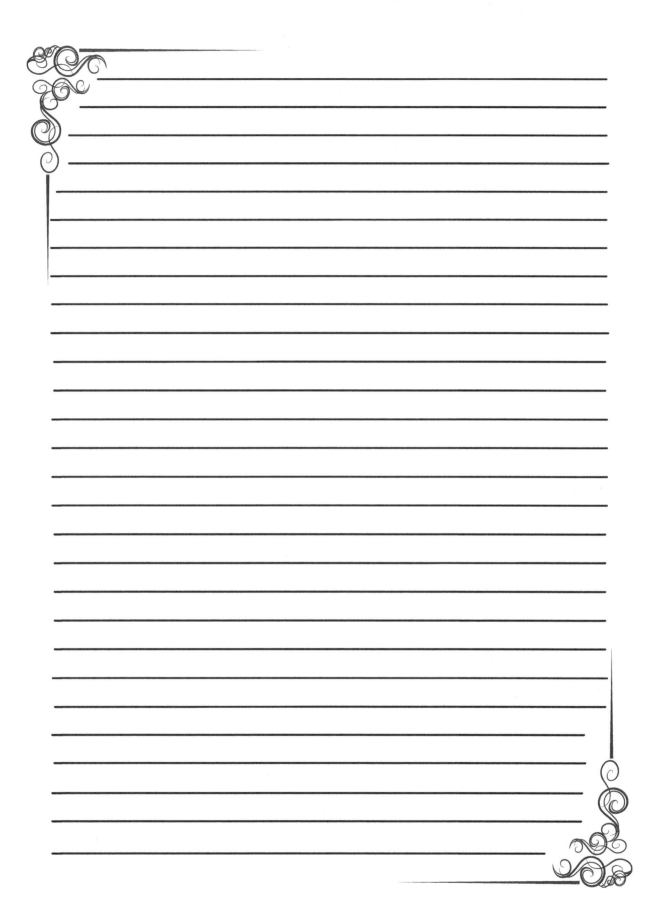

Date: _____

Spirit:

All praise to God, the Father of our Lord Jesus Christ, who has blessed us with every spiritual blessing in the heavenly realms because we are united with Christ. Ephesians 1:3 NLT

Today, for me, this means:

_____

_____

_____

_____

Soul: Today I will feed my soul by:

_____

_____

_____

_____

Body: Today I will feed by body by:

_____

_____

_____

_____

Date: _____

Spirit:

Can two people walk together without agreeing on the direction? Amos 3:3 NLT

Today, for me, this means:

_____

_____

_____

_____

_____

Soul: Today I will feed my soul by:

_____

_____

_____

Body: Today I will feed by body by:

_____

_____

_____

_____

_____

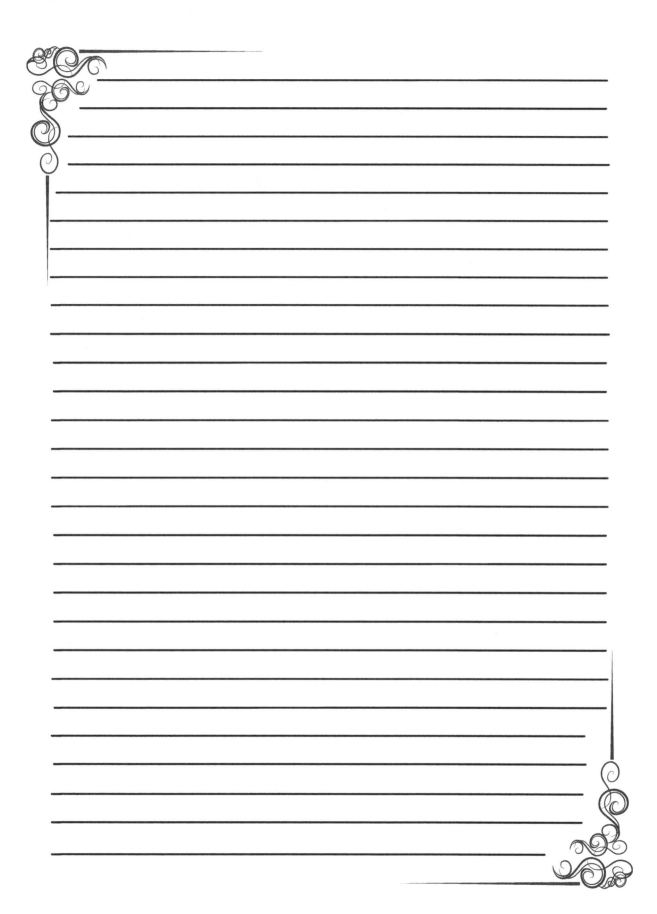

Date: _____

Spirit:

Take delight in the Lord, and he will give you your heart's desires. Psalm 37:4 NLT

Today, for me, this means:

_____
_____
_____
_____
_____

Soul: Today I will feed my soul by:

_____
_____
_____

Body: Today I will feed by body by:

_____
_____
_____
_____
_____

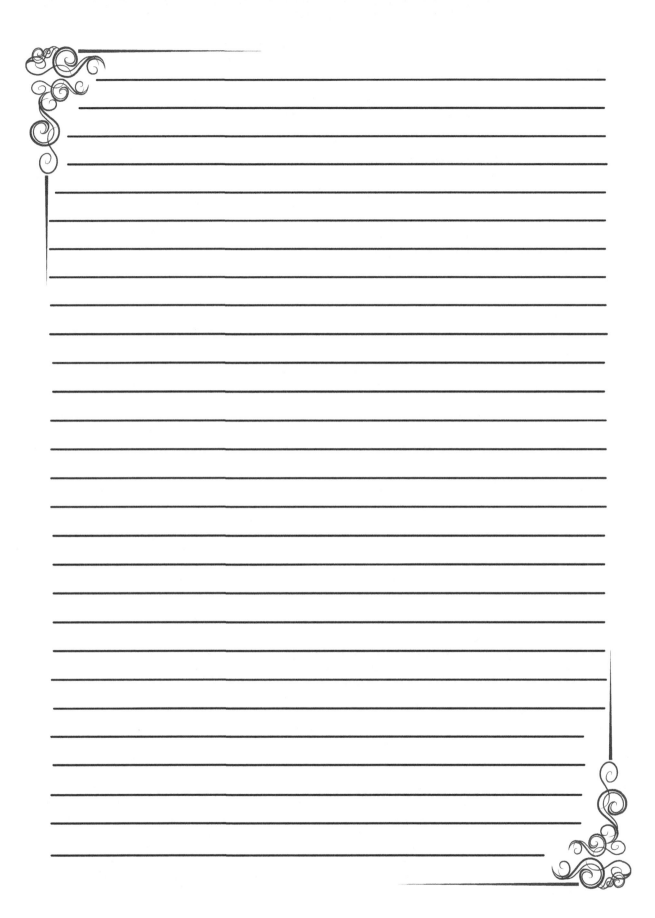

Date: _____

❖ ——— • ——— ❖

As iron sharpens iron, so a friend sharpens a friend.

Proverbs 27:17 NLT

❖ ——— • ——— ❖

Today, for me, this means:

_____
_____
_____
_____
_____

Soul: Today I will feed my soul by:

_____
_____
_____

Body: Today I will feed by body by:

_____
_____
_____
_____

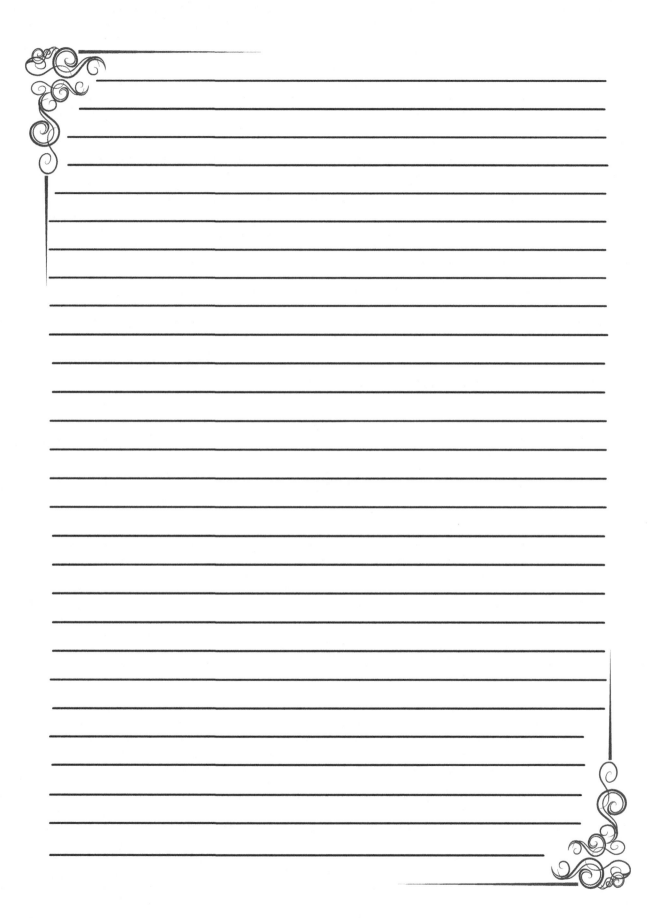

Date: _____

Spirit:

Instead, you must worship Christ as Lord of your life. And if someone asks about your hope as a believer, always be ready to explain it. 1 Peter 3:15 NLT

Today, for me, this means:

_____
_____
_____
_____
_____

Soul: Today I will feed my soul by:

_____
_____
_____
_____

Body: Today I will feed by body by:

_____
_____
_____
_____
_____

Date: _____

Those who are wise will shine as bright as the sky, and those who lead many to righteousness will shine like the stars forever. Daniel 12:3 NLT

Today, for me, this means:

_____

_____

_____

_____

_____

_____

Soul: Today I will feed my soul by:

_____

_____

_____

_____

Body: Today I will feed by body by:

_____

_____

_____

_____

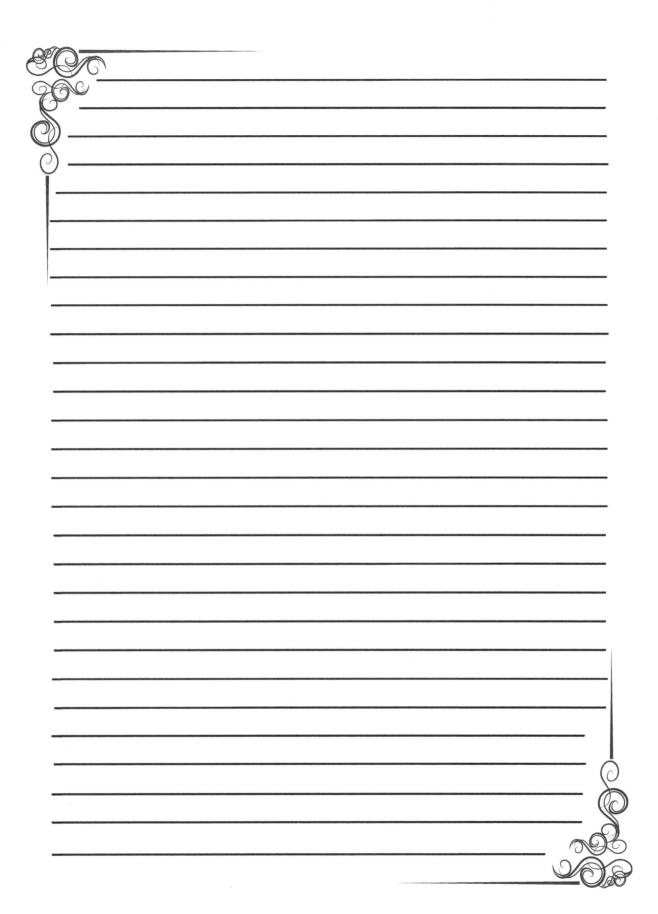

Date: _____

Spirit:

"I am the Alpha and the Omega—the beginning and the end," says the Lord God. "I am the one who is, who always was, and who is still to come—the Almighty One." Revelations 1:8 NLT

Today, for me, this means:

_____
_____
_____
_____

Soul: Today I will feed my soul by:

_____
_____
_____

Body: Today I will feed by body by:

_____
_____
_____
_____

Date: _____

Spirit:

"'You must love the Lord your God with all your heart, all your soul, all your strength, and all your mind.' And, 'Love your neighbor as yourself.'"

Luke 10:27 NLT

Today, for me, this means:

_____

_____

_____

_____

Soul: Today I will feed my soul by:

_____

_____

_____

_____

Body: Today I will feed by body by:

_____

_____

_____

_____

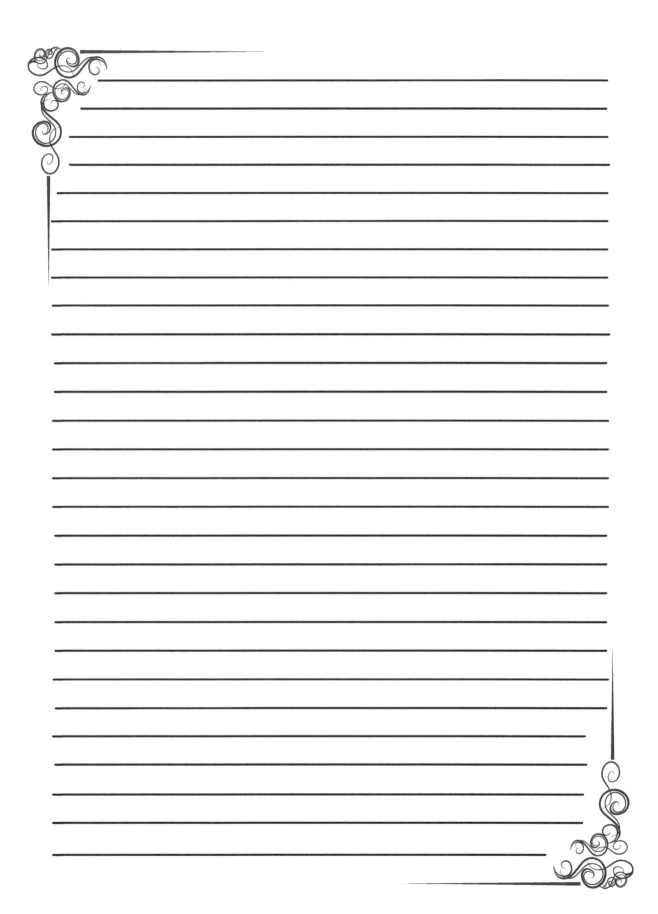

Date: _____

Spirit:

If you need wisdom, ask our generous God, and he will give it to you. He will not rebuke you for asking. Romans 1:5 NLT

Today, for me, this means:

_____
_____
_____

_____
_____
_____

Soul: Today I will feed my soul by:

_____
_____
_____

Body: Today I will feed by body by:

_____
_____
_____
_____

Date: _____

No, O people, the Lord has told you what is good, and this is what he
requires of you: to do what is right, to love mercy, and to walk humbly
with your God. Micah 6:8 NLT

Today, for me, this means:

_____
_____
_____
_____

Soul: Today I will feed my soul by:

_____
_____
_____

Body: Today I will feed by body by:

_____
_____
_____
_____

Date: _____

Spirit:

— ◆ —

For I am convinced that neither death nor life, neither angels nor demons, neither the present nor the future, nor any powers, neither height nor depth, nor anything else in all creation, will be able to separate us from the love of God that is in Christ Jesus our Lord.. Romans 8:38-39

— ◆ —

Today, for me, this means:

_____

_____

_____

_____

Soul: Today I will feed my soul by:

_____

_____

_____

_____

Body: Today I will feed by body by:

_____

_____

_____

_____

_____

Date: _____

<u>Spirit:</u>

Give all your worries and cares to God, for he cares about you.

1 Peter 5:7 NLT

Today, for me, this means:

_____
_____
_____

_____
_____
_____

<u>Soul:</u> Today I will feed my soul by:

_____
_____
_____
_____

<u>Body:</u> Today I will feed by body by:

_____
_____
_____
_____

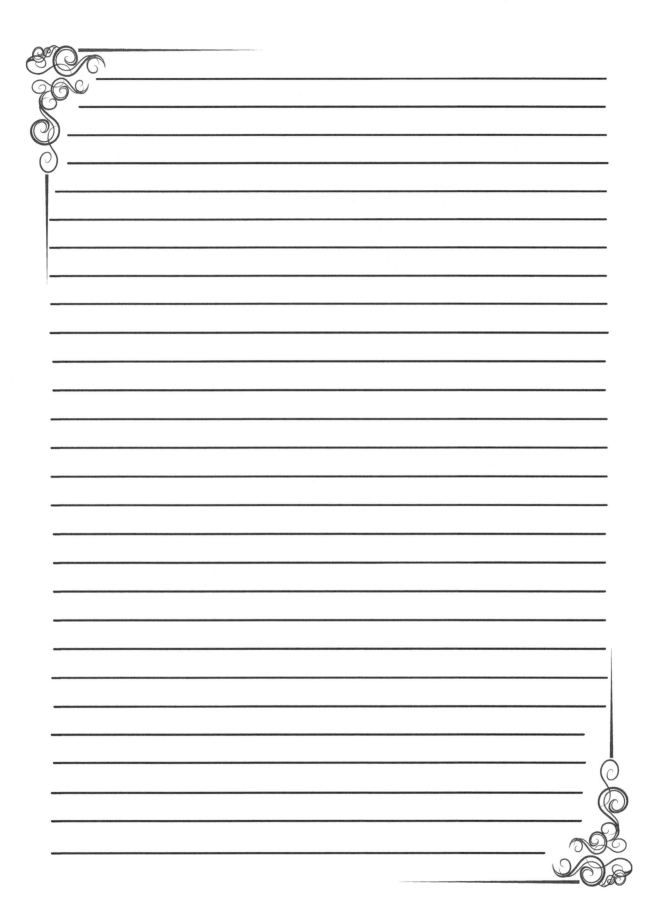

Date: _____

So you see, faith by itself isn't enough. Unless it produces good deeds, it is dead and useless. James 2:17 NLT

Today, for me, this means:

_____
_____
_____

_____
_____
_____

Soul: Today I will feed my soul by:

_____
_____
_____
_____

Body: Today I will feed by body by:

_____
_____
_____
_____

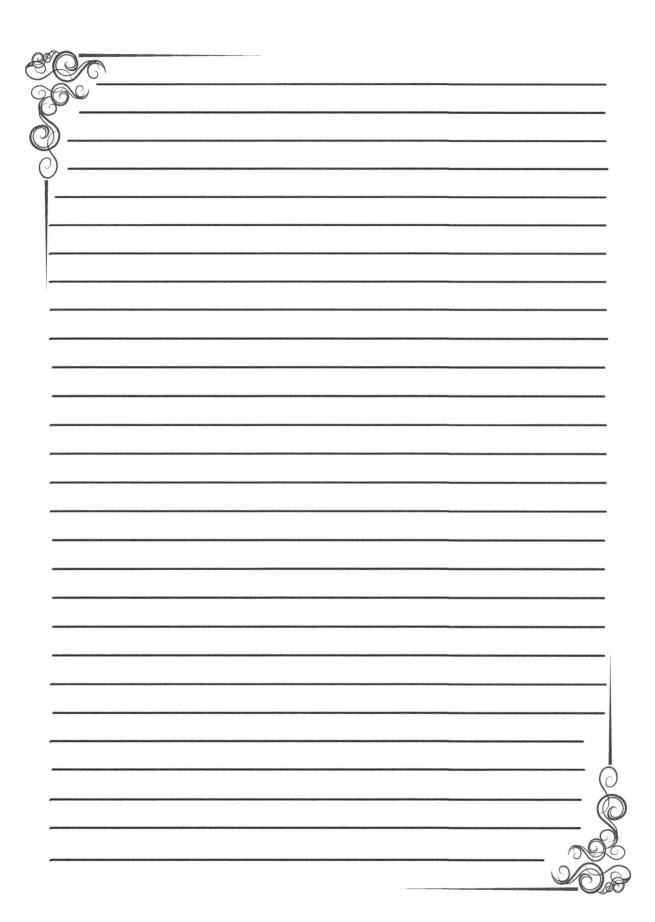

Date: _____

Spirit:

*Three things will last forever—faith, hope, and love—
and the greatest of these is love. 1 Corinthians 13:13 NLT*

Today, for me, this means:

_____
_____
_____

_____
_____

Soul: Today I will feed my soul by:

_____
_____
_____

_____

Body: Today I will feed by body by:

_____
_____
_____
_____
_____

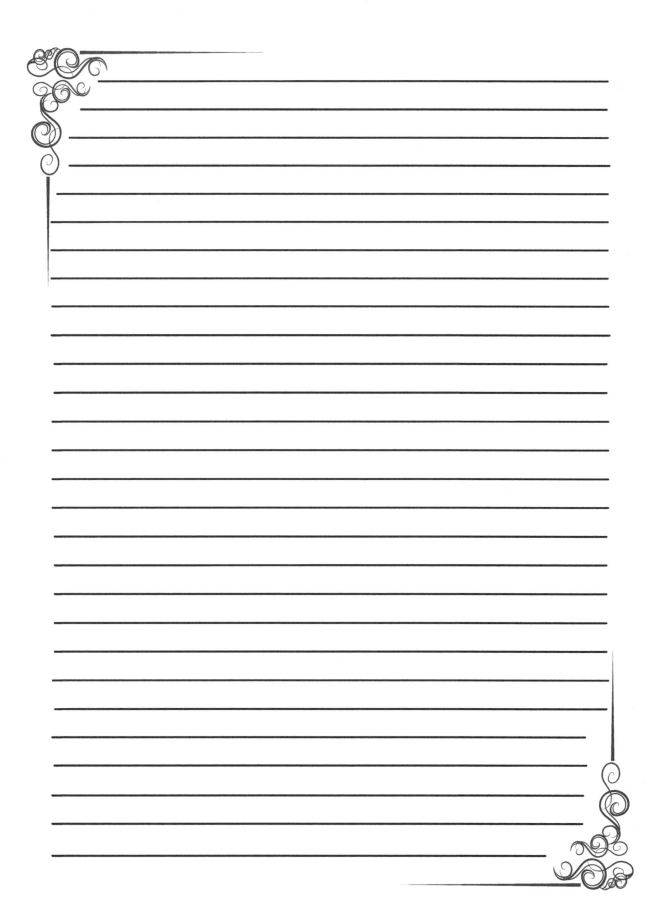

Date: _____

Spirit:

The Lord is my light and my salvation—so why should I be afraid? The Lord is my fortress, protecting me from danger. Psalm 27:1 NLT

Today, for me, this means:

_____
_____
_____

_____

_____

Soul: Today I will feed my soul by:

_____

_____

_____

Body: Today I will feed by body by:

_____
_____
_____
_____
_____

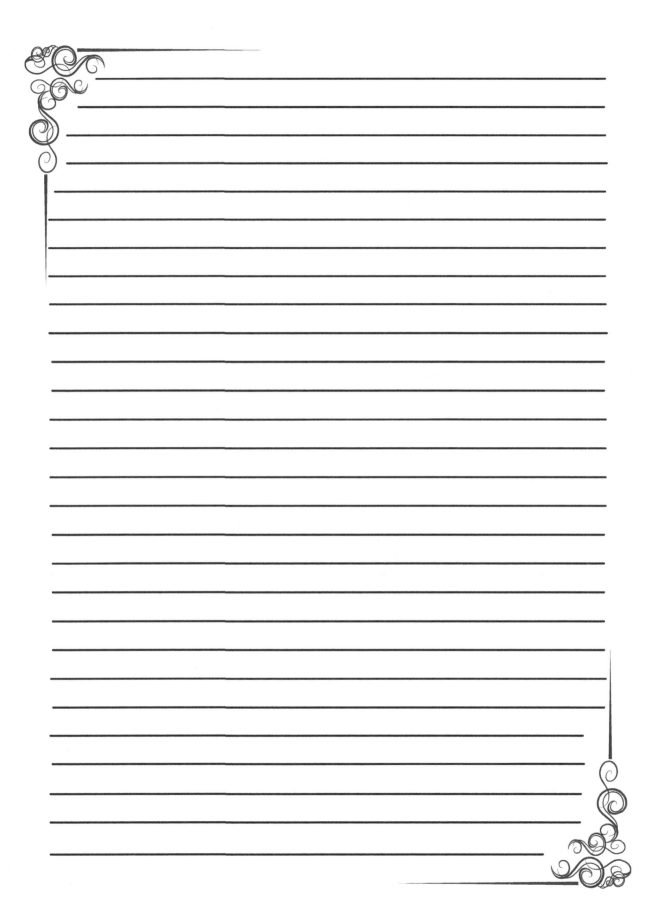

Date: _____

———— ● ————

He will wipe every tear from their eyes, and there will be no
more death or sorrow or crying or pain. All these things are gone,
forever. Revelation 21:4 NLT

———— ● ————

Today, for me, this means:

_____
_____
_____
_____

Soul: Today I will feed my soul by:

_____
_____
_____
_____

Body: Today I will feed by body by:

_____
_____
_____
_____

Date: _____

Spirit:

For we are God's masterpiece. He has created us anew in Christ Jesus, so we can do the good things he planned for us long ago. Ephesians 2:10 NLT

Today, for me, this means:

_____

_____

_____

_____

_____

Soul: Today I will feed my soul by:

_____

_____

_____

Body: Today I will feed by body by:

_____

_____

_____

_____

Date: _____

Spirit:

If any of you wants to be my follower, you must give up your own way, take up your cross daily, and follow me. Luke 9:23 NLT

Today, for me, this means:

_____
_____
_____

_____
_____
_____

Soul: Today I will feed my soul by:

_____
_____
_____

_____

Body: Today I will feed by body by:

_____
_____
_____
_____

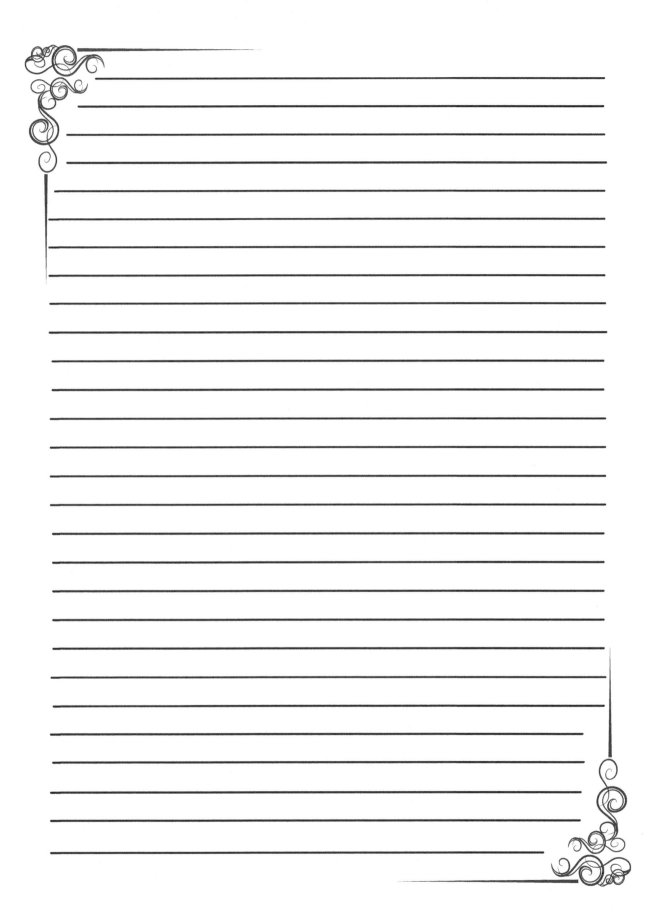

Date: _____

Spirit:

So humble yourselves before God. Resist the devil, and he will flee from you. James 4:7 NLT

Today, for me, this means:

_____

_____

_____

_____

_____

_____

Soul: Today I will feed my soul by:

_____

_____

_____

_____

Body: Today I will feed by body by:

_____

_____

_____

_____

_____

Date: _____

Spirit:

He makes me lie down in green pastures,

he leads me beside quiet waters, he refreshes my

soul. Psalms 23:2-3 NIV

Today, for me, this means:

_____

_____

_____

_____

Soul: Today I will feed my soul by:

_____

_____

_____

Body: Today I will feed by body by:

_____

_____

_____

_____

_____

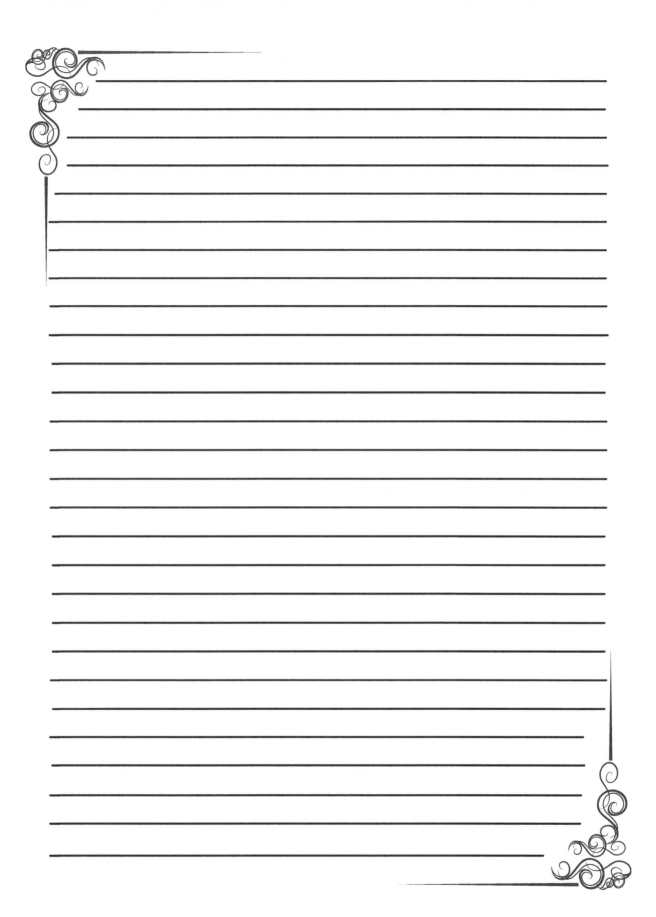

Date: _____

Spirit:

———— •◆• ————

Now may the Lord of peace himself give you his peace at all times and in every situation. The Lord be with you all. 2 Thessalonians 3:16 NLT

———— •◆• ————

Today, for me, this means:

_____

_____

_____

_____

_____

_____

Soul: Today I will feed my soul by:

_____

_____

_____

Body: Today I will feed by body by:

_____

_____

_____

_____

Date: _____

Now this is what the Lord Almighty says, "Give careful thought to your ways." Haggai 1:5 NIV

Today, for me, this means:

_____

_____

_____

_____

_____

Soul: Today I will feed my soul by:

_____

_____

_____

_____

Body: Today I will feed by body by:

_____

_____

_____

_____

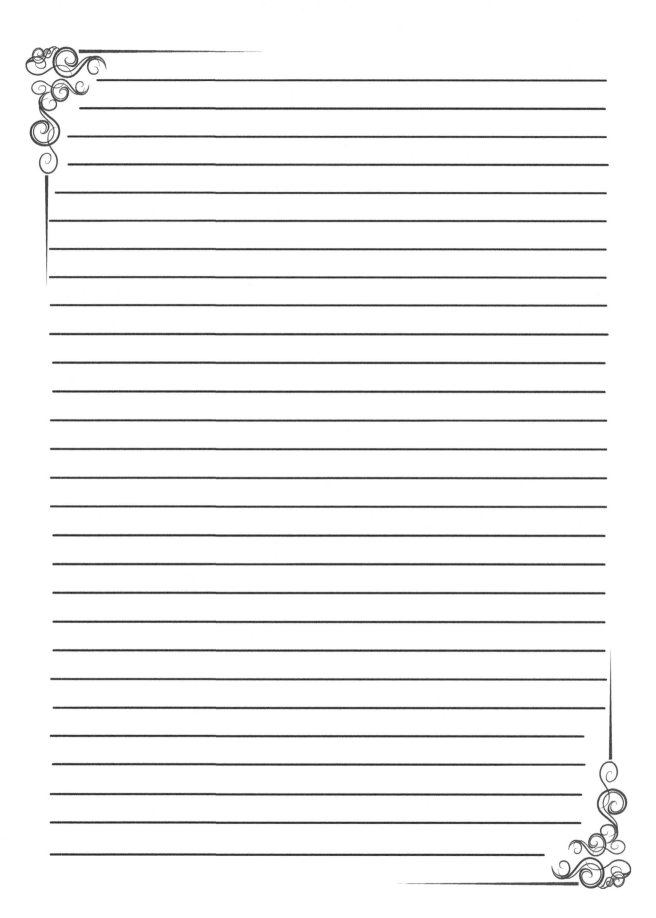

Date: _____

Commit your actions to the Lord, and your plans will succeed.

Proverbs 16:3 NLT

Today, for me, this means:

_____
_____
_____
_____
_____

Soul: Today I will feed my soul by:

_____
_____
_____
_____

Body: Today I will feed by body by:

_____
_____
_____
_____
_____

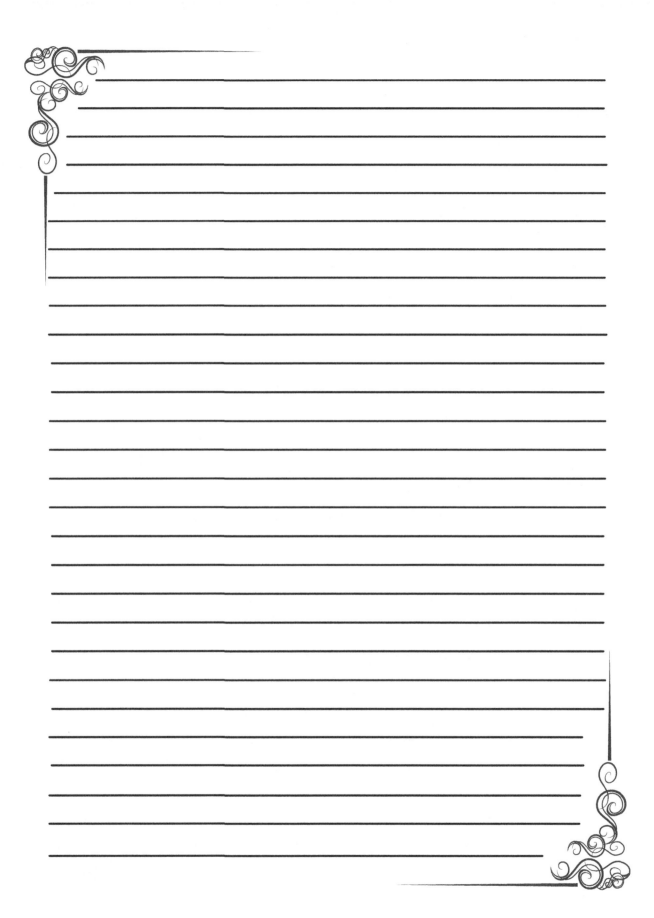

Date: _____

Spirit:

Whatever is good and perfect is a gift coming down to us from God our Father, who created all the lights in the heavens. He never changes or casts a shifting shadow. James 1:17 NLT

Today, for me, this means:

_____

_____

_____

_____

_____

Soul: Today I will feed my soul by:

_____

_____

_____

_____

Body: Today I will feed by body by:

_____

_____

_____

_____

Date: _____

Spirit:

But people who aren't spiritual can't receive these truths from God's Spirit. It all sounds foolish to them and they can't understand it, for only those who are spiritual can understand what the Spirit means. 1 Cor 2:14 NLT

Today, for me, this means:

_____
_____
_____
_____
_____

Soul: Today I will feed my soul by:

_____
_____
_____
_____

Body: Today I will feed by body by:

_____
_____
_____
_____
_____

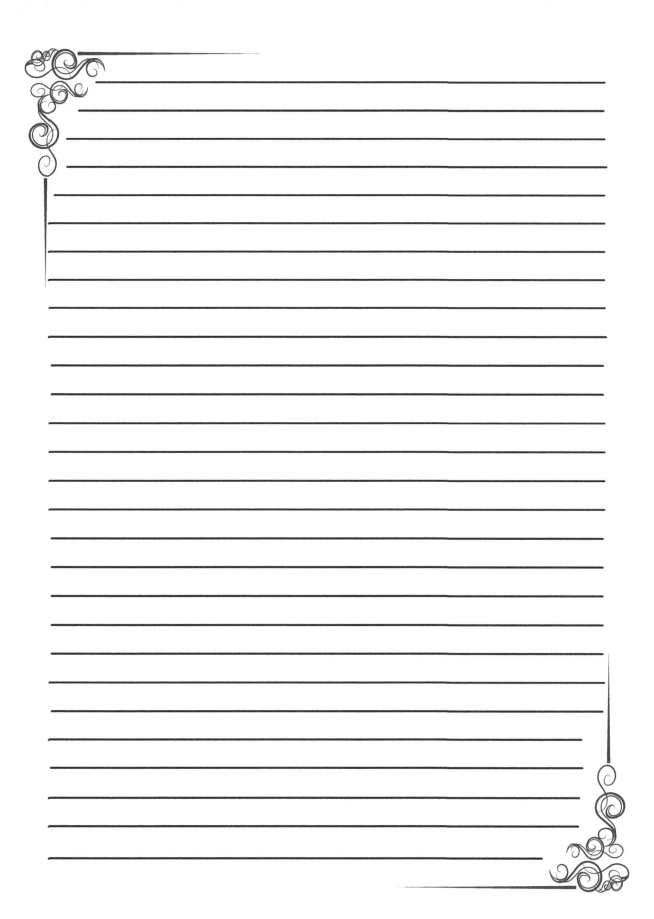

Date: _____

Spirit:

Children are a gift from the Lord; they are a reward from him. Psalm 127:3 NLT

Today, for me, this means:

_____
_____
_____
_____
_____
_____

Soul: Today I will feed my soul by:

_____
_____
_____
_____

Body: Today I will feed by body by:

_____
_____
_____
_____
_____

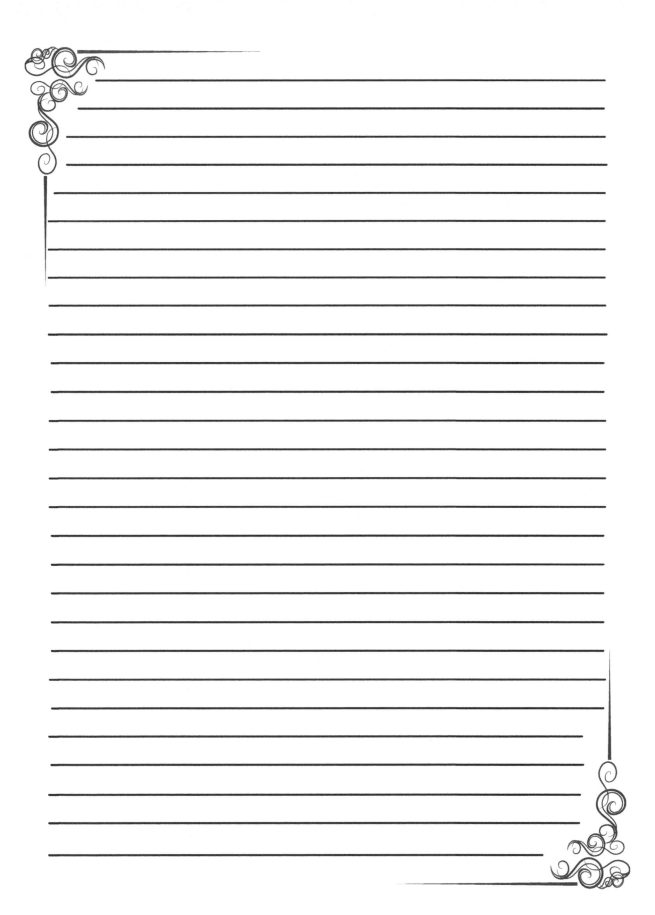

Date: _____

Spirit: _____

But the Lord is faithful; he will strengthen you and guard
you from the evil one. 2 Thessalonians 3:3 NLT

Today, for me, this means:

_____

_____

_____

_____

_____

_____

Soul: Today I will feed my soul by:

_____

_____

_____

_____

Body: Today I will feed by body by:

_____

_____

_____

_____

_____

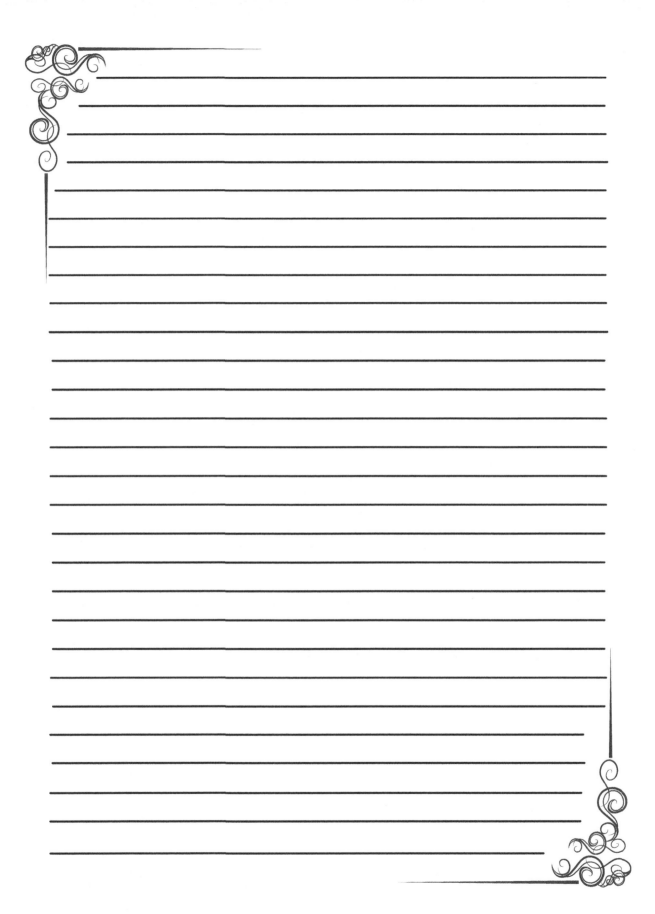

Date: _____

Spirit:

Your word is a lamp to guide my feet and a light for my path.
Psalm 119:105 NLT

Today, for me, this means:

_____
_____
_____
_____
_____
_____

Soul: Today I will feed my soul by:

_____
_____
_____

Body: Today I will feed by body by:

_____
_____
_____
_____

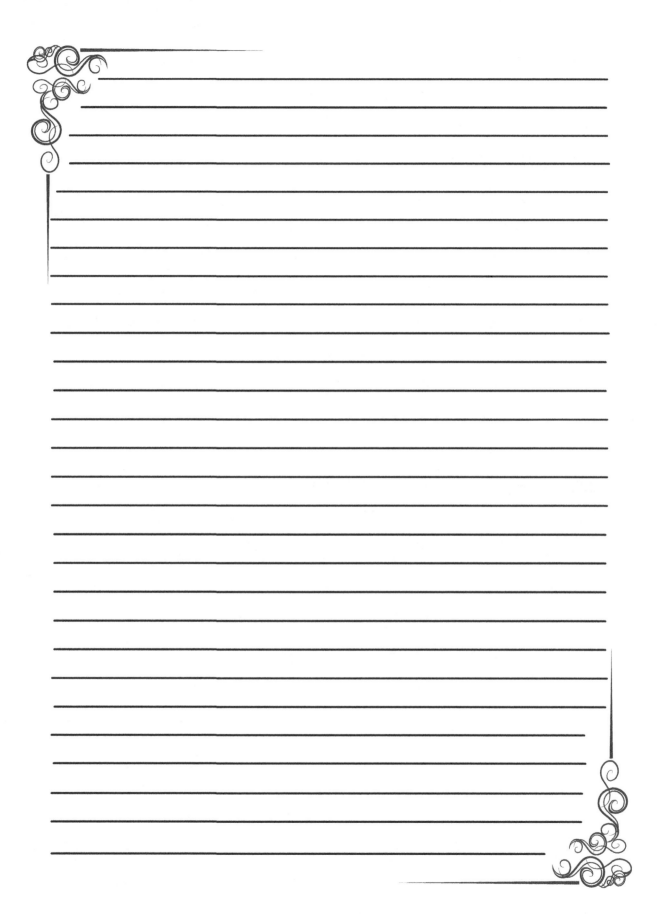

Date: _____

Look! I stand at the door and knock. If you hear my voice and open the door, I will come in, and we will share a meal together as friends.
Revelations 3:20 NLT

Today, for me, this means:

_____

_____

_____

_____

Soul: Today I will feed my soul by:

_____

_____

_____

Body: Today I will feed by body by:

_____

_____

_____

_____

_____

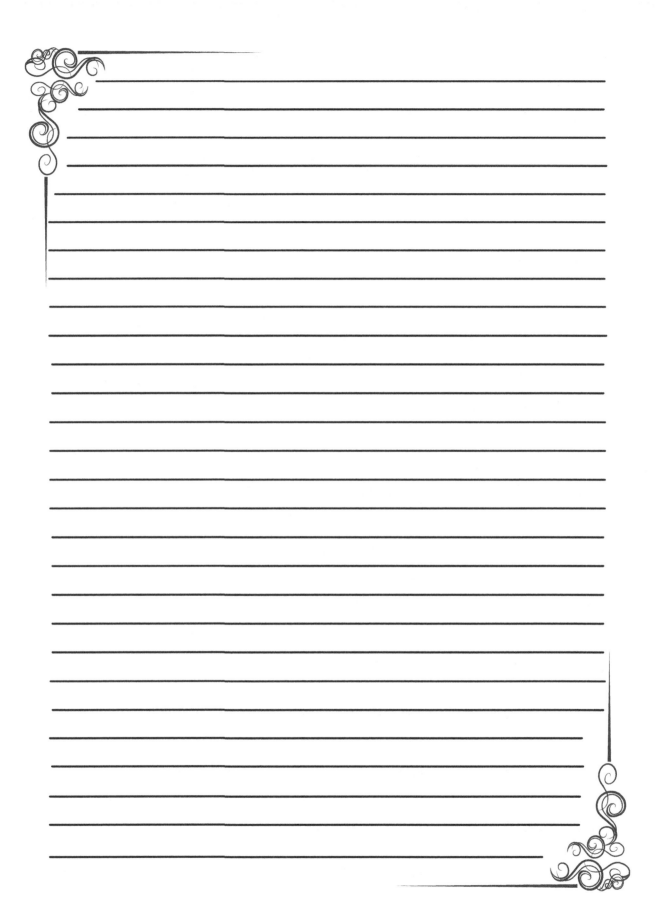

Date: _____

But to you who are willing to listen, I say, love your enemies!
Do good to those who hate you. Luke 6:27 NLT

Today, for me, this means:

_____
_____
_____

_____
_____
_____

Soul: Today I will feed my soul by:

_____
_____
_____

Body: Today I will feed by body by:

_____
_____
_____
_____

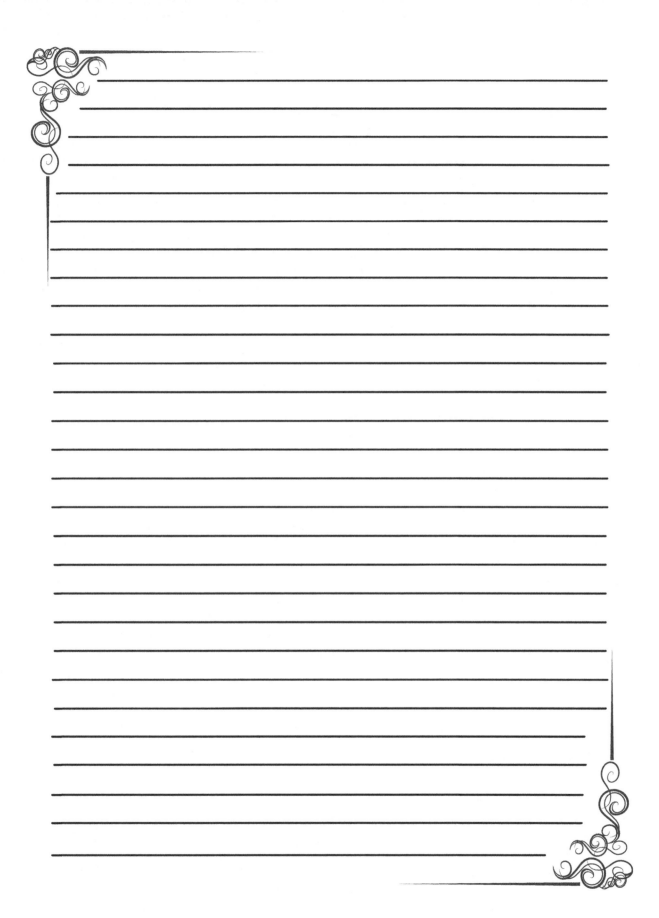

Date: _____

Spirit:

But you are not like that, for you are a chosen people. You are royal priests, holy nation, God's very own possession. As a result, you can show others the goodness of God, for he called you out of the darkness into his wonderful light. 1 Peter 2:9 NLT

Today, for me, this means:

_____

_____

_____

_____

Soul: Today I will feed my soul by:

_____

_____

_____

Body: Today I will feed by body by:

_____

_____

_____

_____

_____

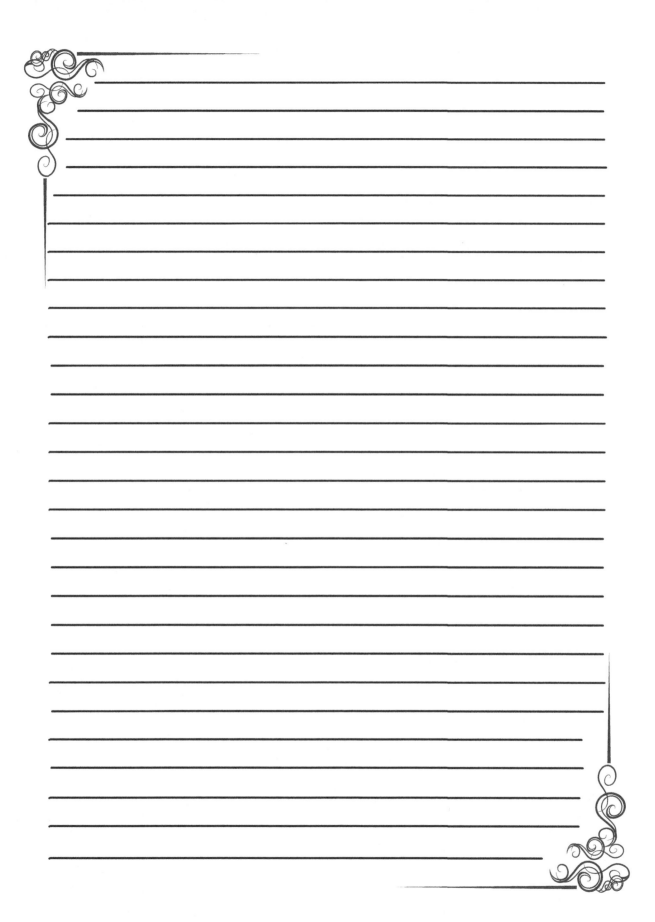

Date: _____

Spirit:

Stay alert! Watch out for your great enemy, the devil. He prowls around like a roaring lion, looking for someone to devour. 1 Peter 5:8 NLT

Today, for me, this means:

_____
_____
_____
_____
_____

Soul: Today I will feed my soul by:

_____
_____
_____

Body: Today I will feed by body by:

_____
_____
_____
_____

Date: _____

Charm is deceptive, and beauty does not last; but a woman who fears the Lord will be greatly praised. Proverbs 31:30 NLT

Today, for me, this means:

_____

_____

_____

_____

_____

_____

Soul: Today I will feed my soul by:

_____

_____

_____

Body: Today I will feed by body by:

_____

_____

_____

_____

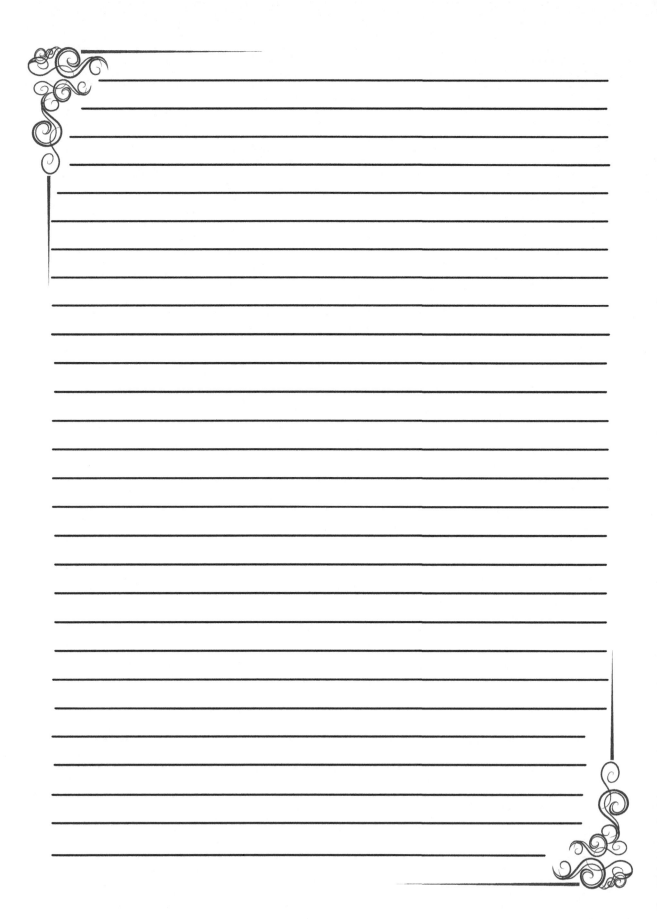

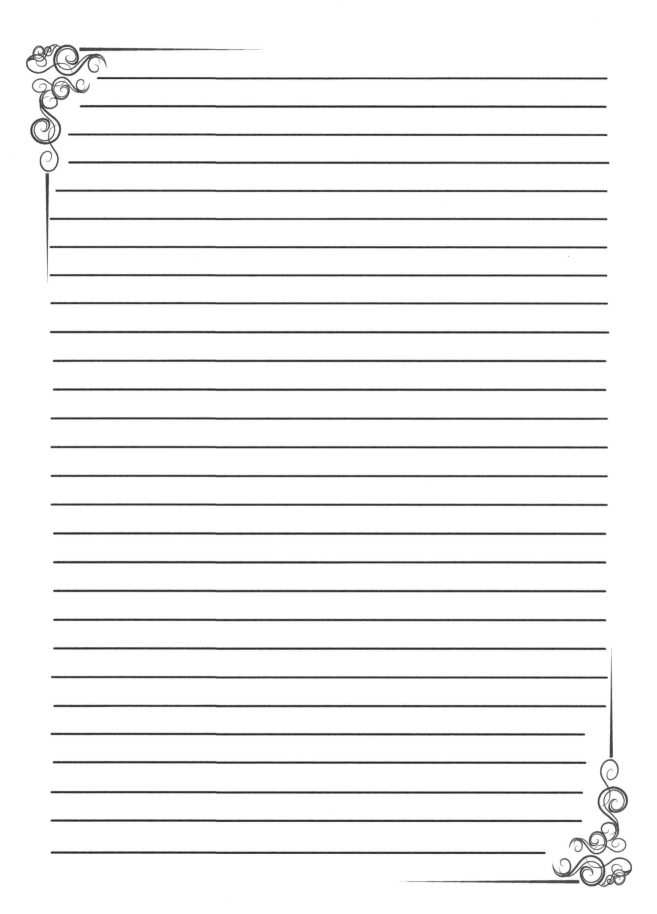

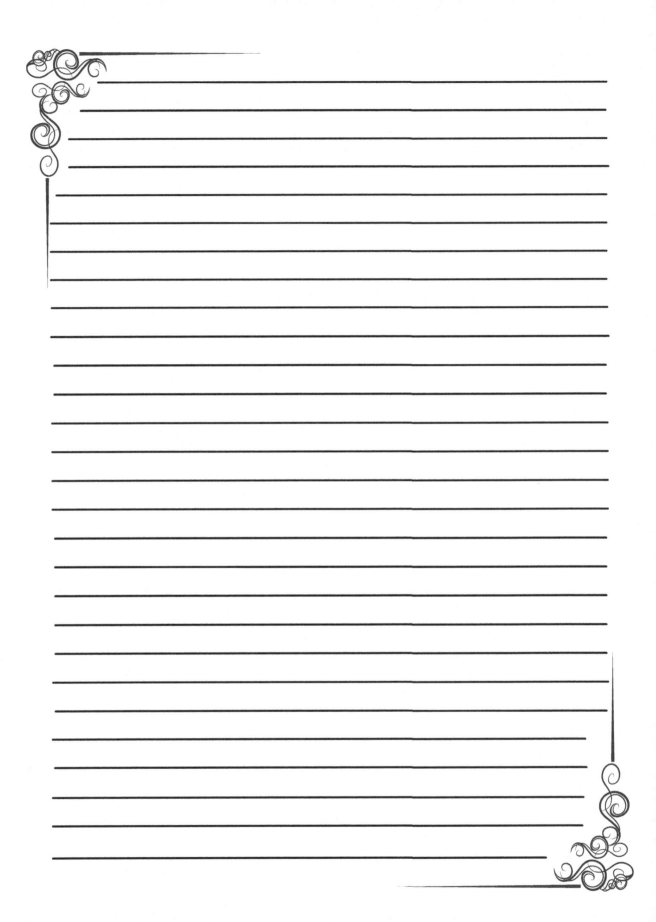

Made in the USA
Middletown, DE
25 April 2022

64767722R00097